More praise for *The Disa*

"A beautifully evocative story of loss."   —*Cleveland Plain Dealer*

"A lyrical and haunting memoir. . . . Jurgensen's is a powerful voice for the unbearable sadness caused by death and the courage and love it takes to live with both the pain of loss and the cherished memories."
—*Kirkus Reviews*

"The successful transformation of a personal tragedy into art is very rare, but Jurgensen has accomplished just that. . . . The power of the writing stems from the author's ability to make every detail immediate."   —*Publishers Weekly* (starred review)

"Sympathetic and intelligent, [*The Disappearance*] shows us not only how the unbearable can be borne, but also that to relieve one's suffering by writing does not diminish love."
—*Evening Standard* (London)

"[A] quietly devastating account. . . . Even readers who are not parents can hardly fail to be moved by the book."
—*The Times* (London)

"Shattering and remarkable thanks to its intelligence and lucidity."
—*Elle*

"This book is beautiful, modest and has a simplicity which is unbearable."   —*Madame Figaro*

"There is not one page, not one sentence, which does not touch your heart."   —*Le Monde*

THE DISAPPEARANCE

GENEVIÈVE JURGENSEN

translated by Adriana Hunter

W. W. Norton & Company
New York   London

First published as a Norton paperback 2000
Copyright © 1994 by Calmann-Lévy
English translation copyright © 1999 by Adriana Hunter
First American edition 1999
Published by arrangement with HarperCollins Publishers Ltd.

Originally published in French as *La Disparition* by Calmann-Lévy in 1994

Manufacturing by The Courier Companies, Inc.

Library of Congress Cataloging-in-Publication Data
Jurgensen, Genevieve, 1946–
    [Disparition. English]
    The disappearance : a memoir of loss / Genevieve Jurgensen ; translated by
Adriana Hunter.
        p. cm.
    ISBN 0-393-04776-8
    1. Jurgenson, Genevieve, 1946–   .—Correspondence. 2. France—Biography.
3. Journalists—France—Correspondence. 4. Loss (Psychology). 5. Children—
Death—Psychological aspects. I. Hunter, Adriana. II. Title.
CT1018.J87 A4   1999
155.9'37'092—dc21
    [B]   99-19426
                                                                                  CIP
    ISBN 0-393-32060-X pbk.

W. W. Norton & Company, Inc., 500 Fifth Avenue, New York, N.Y. 10110
www.wwnorton.com

W. W. Norton & Company Ltd., 10 Coptic Street, London WC1A 1PU

1 2 3 4 5 6 7 8 9 0

to Francine Cicurel

Shortly, very shortly after our daughters were separated from us, and were thrust at such a tender age into infinity, where suddenly they had more in common with the most ancient of the deceased than with their father and mother, close friends predicted: 'you will write it.' I felt a shiver of revulsion run through me. To write was to give life some sort of form in order to suffer less. Suffering was the last way in which I could love my children. I wanted to wash myself of this sentence as if it had been an evil spell.

Later, during the course of my campaign against delinquent driving, I was often talked into giving my testimony. But as the years went by a mystery carved itself out: in the happy, active, rich and all-in-all enviable life that I was leading, what imprint had been left by Mathilde and Elise? A few days after their death, trudging through the rain between the towers of the 15th arrondissement of Paris, a friend and I saw a scrawny dog go by, slinking along the walls of the buildings. 'You see, even that dog wouldn't want my life,' I said to her, and she closed her eyes for a moment. I would not say that any more now. But then, what would I say?

I have tried to write it, in one form, and then another,

for eight years. The more I wrote, the more I felt as if I
were lying. Because writing is solitary, whereas I was not.
I have never been alone. All the same, I could feel people
listening more attentively when I spoke of my two elder
daughters. I ended up writing these letters to one of these
listeners. I have not checked how accurate my memories
were: they are what is left, not what was.

This friend, a television director and historian, had
some idea of work in which I was engaged: reconstituting
something from archives, vestiges which needed to be
endowed with life, which needed checking to find the
truth. Because he paints he was also fully aware of the
appalling distance that constantly separates an author
from his or her subject. He was close enough (we had
met him eight years earlier) and distanced enough (we
had not known him when we still had our first two
daughters) and he was happy to be sent these letters. He
knew that on his support and his reactions, on the least
nuance in his remarks, hung the next letter.

One day last summer he pointed out to me that the
letters were becoming like a personal diary. It was then
that I felt I had finished: I had come back to the life I
lead now.

For every human being, the separation inflicted by the
death of those without whom we would never have
wanted to live is an enigma; I was of course incapable of
resolving it, but I wanted to expose its terms. Life is the
only way of talking about death, which itself always
evades our understanding: so I have talked about my life
over a two-year period, as if through a series of sketches
in black and white I have drawn a portrait of myself. I

could – and would have liked to – pursue this
correspondence for another twenty or thirty years.
Perhaps I will be able to. But these letters will always be
incomplete. Like our family and like our understanding of
our fate.

Long ago, I was a student of Bruno Bettelheim*. The
last time we saw each other was at Santa Monica; he had
recently been widowed and was in a state of deep clinical
depression. We talked at length. He was so sad! He told
me about it. 'I know . . .' I said and I put my hand on his
arm. It was the first time I had touched him. He laughed
and shrugged his shoulders: 'What do you know, you're
so young!' Then he looked at me and said: 'Do you see,
even though I'm old I want to know if I'm going to get
out of this depression and how I'm going to go about it.'

On that point I now resemble my former professor. I
live to understand, and I understand to live.

---

* A philosopher and psychological theorist, most famous for his work
in child psychology, but who has also written about the psychology of
depression and of the Holocaust.

4 December 1991

You never knew our daughters, neither did you know me as I was when they were alive. I will have to tell you everything. Can one really tell someone about very young children? I will not even show you photographs of them. All they show are two little girls, barely distinguishable from each other, just like all the little blond children which people primary school classes and the beaches along the Atlantic coast in the summer. The photographs that I prefer are not necessarily those on which their features are most faithfully reproduced, nor even the most recent, but those which reveal the life we led. In one (I do not know any longer who took it nor where I have put it), Mathilde is two. It is summer, I am pregnant. She is wearing a Greek dress brought back by my mother, I am dressed up in some ample smock. We are neither of us at our best, her straight hair is a bit too long, badly cut, and I have once again let myself get too fat. But we are talking to each other. We are sitting next to each other on the sofa, looking at each other, she is telling me something and I am listening to her, ready to answer, my eyebrows raised. In another photo, in colour this time and taken by Laurent from quite a distance, I am sitting in the shade in the garden as we do in Uzès after lunch. Elise is on my lap; crushed against me and turning her back to the photographer. Over her shoulder I am reading a Tintin book. She is wearing just a little checked swimming costume, I myself am wearing a long Provençal skirt, a flimsy white shirt ordered from a catalogue and espadrilles. I threw that skirt out last summer. But I still have many clothes from that time.

On the 29th of April 1980 the official photographer for the school which my daughters attended came to take some class photographs. They were both dead the next day, indeed we did not receive these photographs until several weeks after the news of our solitude. Mathilde's class is in uniform, so it is a picture of a little girl in navy blue in a row, stifling her giggles in between her best friends. Elise, who was still in the nursery class, is wearing the dress with the sailor collar that my mother gave her. She is sitting in the first row, looking solemnly at the lens. I think that in this picture she is really very like me.

In Mathilde's satchel, which I keep at Uzès, I still have her school overall with her name embroidered on it, with its ink stains and biscuit crumbs in the pockets. In her exercise book, in her childish but careful handwriting, she has written the date which will be the date of her death and the death of her little sister: *Wednesday, 30 April 1980.*

What else can I tell you? I would like you to have heard me talking to them just once, even if only on the telephone. I feel powerless in trying to make you accept this evidence: they were here, I was their mother. I went to pick them up at school. We stopped at the

supermarket to buy two cheap waxed coats, one in red,
one in blue, and I dropped them off with my mother, not
before playing a practical joke on her on the landing: I
bundled my daughters up in the coats with the hoods up,
pulled tightly over their noses and tied under their chins.
They rang the bell and I hid, and my mother pretended
not to recognize them. Then I went home, because I was
a speech therapist at the time, and I had patients waiting.
My sister-in-law came as intended to pick Mathilde and
Elise up to take them to their other grandmother, but
they never arrived because they died towards the end of
the afternoon, about ten metres from each other, on the
side of the *Autoroute du Nord*. In the meantime, I had
spoken to them once more on the telephone.

6 December 1991

I am hesitating about what to write next. There is no
common ground between before and after, or at least
what they have in common strikes me as just as painful to
excavate as the most deeply buried relics of before.

Yes, I am hesitating. I would like to tell you something
else about my daughters, putting off the inevitable
moment when I will tell you how we learned of their
death. You already know about their end but what do you
know of their beginnings? When I have told you that one
was more blond and slender, the other more athletic and
with darker hair and skin, we will be a lot further on! We
were living at Auteuil in the apartment that you knew.
Sometimes in that neighbourhood I come across a little
girl in blue gabardine holding hands with her little sister
who is scurrying along beside her: even now I have to
look at them to check that it is not Mathilde and Elise.

I am afraid of failing. I am afraid that you will believe
more readily in their death than in their lives. I would
like it if just once when you are reading my letters, if just
once you missed them. If I could achieve that . . . A few
years ago I still used to drive out into the countryside and
bellow at the top of my lungs: 'Mathilde!' I was really
calling her. It would not have really surprised me if my

eldest daughter had appeared in her denim dungarees and
her checked shirt at the end of the dirt track. Of course
she did not come. At least I had spoken her name once
more. Sometimes I meet a little girl who has the same
name as her, and I speak it. I say: 'Hello, Mathilde,
goodbye, Mathilde' with a smile and I think: 'Help, help.'

Simone Veil* says that if the prisoners said nothing
when they were released from concentration camps it was
because those around them had no desire to hear their
stories. As often as I feel that people have a sincere and
kindly-meant curiosity about our story, I also feel their
sad indifference to the lives of two children who were no
more special than any other you might film in the places
that children of four and seven are found: in the square,
at the zoo, or queuing up to see a film. A friend who I
thought had never known them disabused me: 'I saw you
one winter's evening crossing the Avenue de Versailles
with them.' He had not called out to me so as not to
trouble me. He said we had seemed to be so 'busy' that
he preferred to watch us from a distance. He had lost
sight of us as we slipped into the little street of the *Les
Trois Murat* cinema, where we were going to see *The
Jungle Book*. It would be enough if you had just glimpsed
me like that, crossing a wide street at night, torn between
my anxiety about the traffic and the rush to avoid missing
the beginning of the film. It would not matter if you
weren't even sure you had recognized me. The most

* French politician and the first President of the European Parliament;
she was herself a survivor of Auschwitz and Bergen-Belsen.

fleeting impression would spare me from having to
convince you of the existence of two creatures who did
not live long enough to lose more than two milk teeth.

undated letter

*O*n the eve of that May Day holiday, we were not expecting anyone to call, and the ringing of the telephone awakened no feelings in us. We lifted the receiver without curiosity.

A slight rustling on the line indicated that the call was being made from outside Paris. My sister? No, I knew she was on her way to Paris. An unfamiliar man's voice checked that we were indeed the people he was looking for, then told us to hold the line. The next voice was that of our brother-in-law, Christian, who had left with his wife, their baby and our two girls. We asked him how he was. He said that he was not good at all, that they had had a very serious car accident. We said: 'Yes? And?' He told us our two little girls were dead. We thought he was playing a joke on us and then thought no-one would play a joke in such poor taste. Laurent said: 'But, Christian, it's not true.' He fell to his knees, calling his children. I asked for news of the others. Everyone was fine. Where did we have to go? 'To the hospital in Péronne.' I did not know where it was; Christian gave us a few directions, Laurent knew. We hung up.

I immediately felt how impossible it was to raise myself to the scale of this event. The terror mounted in me out

of all proportion to my own dimensions. I could not
contain it all. It was expanding and expanding and I was
not. I was still this little woman in her little apartment,
next to a little man in the same little apartment. The
terror targeted us exclusively, we were its only prey, its
only destination, the terminus; it was a giant and we were
dwarves. Laurent took me by the wrists and asked me not
to scream. He said: 'To think we're going to have to get
over this.'

A big part of us has stayed there for ever. I will tell
you what happened next, everything you want to know
about what happened next. But at the moment I cannot.
Just as then, I am looking for the link between my
daughters and that news.

We had to go to Péronne. We could not drive. What
did we want to go to Péronne for? What was there there
that was of any use to us? The maternal reflexes were
working by themselves. My eyes were turning towards the
bookshelves where I kept their Health Records. The
Health Records! In navy blue! To write what in them?
Their school reports? The social security cards? The
family record book. There. They would surely need the
family record book.

Someone was ringing the doorbell. We made our way
to the door, terrified, clinging to each other. It was
Christian's mother. She had come to get us with one of
her other sons.

We sat ourselves down in the back of their car.

undated letter

*Y*ou tell me that I am proceeding in concentric circles.
I would like to proceed in eccentric circles! To distance
myself from that telephone call taken in our apartment as
we were getting ready to go to the cinema. I was looking
at myself in the mirror when the telephone rang. For the
first time since Elise was born we had let ourselves be
convinced: we were going away without the girls for a
business trip. I was asking for Laurent's opinion on the
blue dress with white polka dots that I had just bought.
The door to the girls' room hung open into the hallway
we were in, where the telephone was too.

I do not want any part of this account. I picked up the
receiver so innocently, do you understand? There was
nothing to warn me. I wanted my husband to think I
looked pretty in my new dress. That's all.

In the summer I used to take the girls to Noirmoutier
where my parents used to take my sister and me at the
same age. One day, Mathilde and Nicholas, my sister's
son, were playing by the water's edge on one of the
'ocean side' beaches, one of those long beaches that
people ride along and where you can never get to the
end. Walking amongst the dunes we disturbed some
nudists, whom Mathilde called dunists. The waves were

too big, the shoreline too steep for children who could
not yet swim, and the seaweed was congregating into a
cloying moving carpet which caressed our ankles
disturbingly. Nicholas was leaping in with shrieks of
delight while Mathilde stood on the edge, rooted to the
spot.

'Come on!' called my nephew.

She did not move.

'Are you frightened of the water?'

'No, I'm not frightened of the water.'

'Are you frightened of the crabs?'

'No, I'm not frightened of the crabs.'

'Are you frightened of the seaweed?'

'No, I'm not frightened of the seaweed.'

'Well, then, what are you afraid of?'

'I'm frightened full stop, that's all.'

Me too, I'm frightened, full stop, that's all. Perhaps I
should tell you about these incidents in person, looking at
you? I would see from your eyes whether I am
communicating to you some of my fear. I would pepper
my sentences with: 'do you understand?' I would think
about each word, I would be discouraged: 'I don't know
how to tell you this . . .'

If you have seen *Platoon*, you will surely remember this
scene: a soldier, a young American recruit, has fallen
asleep despite his best efforts while he is on watch. When
he wakes up in the night it is misty and he scans the
darkness. His friends are asleep. Who lives in that
darkness, that fog? Who animates the moist foliage? He
is reduced to himself in a country, a climate, a vegetation
which are not his own. Danger is upon him, but where

and what form does it take? It is war. War is going to
come out of the darkness, the mist and the leaves. War is
cleaving through the jungle with a rustling of vegetation.
He looks and looks. And all of a sudden, the Vietnamese
are there. They really are on him.

When that telephone rang, like soldiers caught sleeping
on duty, we too scoured the silence of the apartment with
our eyes.

undated letter

*I*n his journal, after killing Luc Taron, Lucien Léger*
writes: 'I am heading for the Seine having gratuitously
killed the most lonely and innocent passer-by.'

You will never hear me compare the death of the two
little ones to a murder. I will make this clearer later if
you like. That sentence of Lucien Léger talks simply and
justly of the moment in our lives that we do not all
experience, the moment when something takes aim at us.
Mathilde and Elise left at exactly the right moment for
Jacques I. to kill them, them and only them. In order for
this to happen, there was an extraordinary accumulation
of concordant circumstances. If just one of them had been
omitted, no-one would have known what sort of disaster
we had escaped. I will tell you about all these

---

* Lucien Léger is France's longest serving and most notorious prisoner.
Aged twenty-nine, he was condemned to life imprisonment – having
narrowly escaped the death penalty – in 1966 for the murder of the
ten-year-old Luc Taron two years previously. He wrote numerous
letters confessing to the murder, saying that he had killed in order to
be famous, and threatening to kill again. What fascinated Jurgensen
about this case and made her draw the comparison was Léger's
completely arbitrary choice of a victim: if the boy had not happened to
be in that place at that time, he would still be alive today.

circumstances. Because their enumeration also tells you
something of the life we led, what connections we had
and the limitations of our power.

The telephone rang in the stillness of the apartment
and we too were chosen as targets. During the course of
the conversation, in the few sentences that it took to
reach the explosion, we realized that the cannons were
adjusting their aim and we had to offer ourselves to their
missiles.

Monday, 6 January 1992

So we left for Péronne. We were huddled together in
the back of the car. Laurent gave me a cigarette, I do not
know where he got it from because we had both given
up smoking years before. A few minutes later my hands
felt cold, there was sweat on my brow and I felt weak;
I told him I felt I was leaving and he replied: 'It's the
smoke.'

I cannot remember whether or not there were any
traffic jams. It seemed a long way to me. We stopped at a
service station to fill up with petrol. Mrs L asked whether
I would like to have something to drink, which I did.
The people in the cafeteria seemed a long way away.

Here and there along the edge of the motorway I
noticed damaged cars. I squeezed Laurent's arm and he
said: 'No, no, it's not theirs.'

We arrived at the door of the hospital. Jean-Bernard
asked where we had to go and the porter replied: 'In
surgery.' Then I thought that my daughters had been
operated on before they died and everything expanded
into infinity again. Corridors. It was difficult to walk. My
sister-in-law at the end of a corridor, arms circling
around her, a room. My brother-in-law, my sister-in-law,
a stranger. They ask us if we would like to see them, if

we wanted to see our daughters. You would have had to
drag me there with a tractor.

They ask us if we would like to ring anyone to let
them know. I then understand that this horror does not
stop at us, that we have to tell my mother. No. It's the
evening. She is not expecting any news this evening. Let
her sleep one more time.

I was right, they need the family record book. When
they ask for it and I reply: 'Yes, we've brought it with us,'
I feel proud for a moment. We are good parents. We
thought of everything.

Aline and Christian are going to spend the night in
hospital near their baby, Aude. All three are kept under
observation.

We are taken back. In fact, we came for nothing.
Right from the first instant, death is this nothing.

Mrs L suggests that we stay the night at her house. I
agree readily. She lost a son long ago. I stay downstairs in
our block while Laurent goes up to get pyjamas and
toothbrushes. I do not want to go back into the
apartment. I think that Laurent would have preferred to
stay there.

At the Ls' house we eat what we are given, food and
sleeping pills.

18 January 1992

It is not so much in words that I am lacking to tell
you all this but in courage. When I realize that I have
forgotten something and I have to retrace my steps, I say
to myself: 'Is it really worth it?'

Before taking the sleeping pill, we thought that over at
La Haye, their grandparents were waiting for our
daughters. Laurent's parents. Have I told you that they
were attending the coronation of Queen Beatrix of
Holland? Have I told you that on the 30th of April 1980
this young woman was rising to the throne, and that, ever
since, this date has been celebrated there as the joyful
anniversary of an event whose secondary effect was the
death of the girls? That my father-in-law, the French
ambassador, and my mother-in-law were attending the
festivities? That all the embassy staff were busy so we had
found no-one to go and fetch the girls at the airport?
That, resigned only at the very last minute, I had
cancelled the places reserved for them on the Air France
flight? Have I told you that at my mother's house, before
they were picked up by their aunt, they had watched the
coronation ceremony on television, as I had done out of
the corner of my eye at home? Have I told you that,
seeing my father-in-law's very characteristic form and

gait, I telephoned my mother to ask whether everyone had spotted him and I can still hear in the background Mathilde's voice full of disappointment: 'No! I didn't see him.' The very, very last time. My mother told me that at the time Elise was turned away from the television, absorbed in her drawing, but that that had not stopped her from affirming energetically: 'But I did, I saw him.' And that Mathilde – intoxicated by the sumptuous spectacle, the beautiful gowns, the jewels, the grandiose music – had audaciously and blushingly said quietly:

'I'd like to be Queen of France when I'm bigger.'

Since then I have not called Mathilde nor Elise. Or if I have called my eldest daughter it was without the hope that she would reply. It was to feel the vibration in my larynx of those syllables chosen when I was twenty-five years old, the arrangement of clear vowels and aquatic consonants which were to name the first of my children, to accompany her all her life, to act as her passport, announce her arrival, to be said with only a hint of shyness and finally – in the mouth of the one who would love her – to betray all the emotions that this girl would one day elicit, that she alone would arouse in one young man, a young man who will never know her, who lives and who does not live to love her.

It had been arranged that my mother-in-law would slip away from the ceremony to get back to the embassy and wait for her daughter, her son-in-law and her three little granddaughters. Only then could she be contacted. But she was alone at the residence. Quite alone next to the children's room that she had arranged with so much more anxious tenderness than we would usually bestow on our

children. Could we really ring her then, when she was
alone? No. It would be better to get hold of my father-
in-law at the Palace in Amsterdam, and to tell him to go
back to his wife. As quickly as possible, because she was
surely beginning to think it was getting late. I do not
now remember how Laurent found the right telephone
numbers. He spoke to his father whom I heard saying:
'Oh shit, oh shit, I love you both, I love you both so
much,' and he had to be persuaded to leave and rejoin his
wife, and he protested in the face of this impossible task:
'She mustn't be told . . .' But how could it be hidden
from her? He set off.

As for my mother, I had made up my mind. I would
ask a couple, some friends (friends of hers, but much
younger than her), to go in the morning, when she
woke, before she had time to try and get hold of
me and ask me about the journey of the 'two little
darlings', as she called them. I therefore called Jean-Paul
and Simone. I woke them up, it must have been
midnight. And I gave them responsibility for their task. I
do not think that I underestimated the magnitude of the
effort it would require. But this was a time for friends to
act heroically

Sleeping pill, then, and bed. I think Mrs L suggested
that I went to spend a penny. I had to be told everything.

When I came to, I was back out in the corridor, the
long corridor of this old apartment in Auteuil which
provided a home for a large family. I felt my way along
the walls, even though the light was on. I was making my
way towards a ringing sound. In the hall Mrs L had just
lifted the handset of the telephone. Seeing me coming,

like a sleepwalker who was acutely lucid, she said to my
mother-in-law: 'Here is Vève.'

My mother-in-law's voice on the telephone. She
wanted some news, she had been waiting a long time.
No-one had arrived. She couldn't understand why I was
staying with the Ls. I told her: 'Christian, Aline and
Aude are fine. But Mathilde and Elise are dead.' She
screamed, she must have moved away from the telephone
because I heard her cries from further away, and then at
the same moment my father-in-law arrived. I went back
to bed, leaning against the walls all the way.

21 January 1992

*W*hen we woke, at around seven in the morning, I
felt the enormity of the town sleeping around me, and I
felt as if I could see in the distance the roofs under which
friends were sleeping, friends I needed to get hold of. I
could not wait. I wanted them to know. I wanted their
telephones to ring, for them to answer them and hear my
voice. I wanted their love to light up like a burning torch.
I wanted them to feel a gushing torrent of despair in the
face of their impotence. I knew who I wanted to ring and
who they in turn had to ring. From house to house, from
street to street, so that everyone knew. So that no-one
was left in ignorance. So that each person for whom the
names Laurent, Geneviève, Mathilde and Elise meant
something would wake and find it difficult to believe the
news I gave them.

First Nathalie. I knew she was in the country. In her
little house in the woods thirty kilometres from Paris, the
woods of our childhood; I rang her. Her husband
answered in a muffled voice. 'Renaud, I'm sorry', and he
said: 'You want to speak to Nathalie.' Her, her. Make her
come to the telephone, quickly, make her come. Then
there was her voice: 'Geneviève?' I told her: 'Nathalie, I've
lost my children . . .' She took a while to understand,

asked me what I meant. She hopes she has misunderstood me. I explain.

We must tell Philippe, Laurent's brother. I do not remember exactly which one of us rang him. Perhaps I did. I think I got hold of his mother-in-law at Palaiseau: it was the May Day bank holiday, no-one was actually at home. Françoise, Philippe's wife, told me later that her mother had come into her room and woken her with these words: 'Françoise, something terrible has happened.' And she immediately thought of her own three sons, and tried to imagine what could have happened to each of them: which one?

Laurent sent a telegram to Morocco, where we were meant to be going. I rang my boss, the psychiatrist I was working with. I asked him whether I had called at an inconvenient time. With a smile contradicting his denial, he said: 'No, go on . . .' I told him that, as my children were dead, I would hope to be in the office on Monday but that I could not be sure, that I was terribly sorry about the possible inconvenience, that I would keep him informed . . . He told me how powerless he felt, and I can remember the note of devastation in his familiar and very deep voice.

Laurent looked at his watch. 'Your mother knows now. I'm going,' he said. He went out on foot, alone, into the deserted streets of the First of May, into the harsh light of that first morning. Later the telephone rang, it was him: 'Do you want to speak to your mother?' 'Yes, straight away! Straight away!' He handed the receiver to her and I heard myself yelping like a puppy: 'Mummy! Mummy!' And she said: 'Do you want me to come over?'

She had to come, that instant, to walk through the door
right now. Mummy, come.

Laurent arrived with her. Jean-Paul and Simone, who
had told her, came too. She came in; she was so little,
and old, and shrunken, stooped in her woollen coat. Oh,
Mummy.

I must tell you about something else. Something
happy, any little anecdote will do. Unless I have to, I do
not want to force myself to stick to the chronology of
what happened eleven years ago. Nearly twelve years,
now.

22 January 1992

*O*n the 20th of October 1972 I gave birth to
Mathilde. Childbirth was still in the dark ages: no
ultrasound scans, no epidurals, no monitoring. Having
been admitted to hospital at night, and Laurent having
been asked to go back home, I stayed alone for hours;
from time to time a brusque nurse would come and tell
me to stop listening to myself, to get up, walk about,
think about something else. Then when the midwives
and doctors arrived at about nine o'clock they shoved
some drip into me to speed up the process, and they took
me to the delivery room. Laurent waited on the other
side of the door. She was born at two o'clock in the
afternoon, and straight away and forever there she was,
Mathilde Jurgensen, my first born daughter, wrapped
up in the little metal cradle next to the bed on which
they were stitching me up. I looked at her, I met her
for the first time, I introduced myself to her. We were
both serious, questioning, consenting. After twelve
hours of exertion, furious that I had suffered so much, I
was nonetheless quite confident. Useless at running,
poorly balanced on my skis, vague with a tennis racket,
incapable of clearing more than one metre in high jump,
frightened of the sea and too quickly worn out on a

bicycle, I had at last found a sport that suited me: giving birth.

They took me back up to the ward and offered me some soup: goodness, those salted vegetables were good! Then my mother came, young, smiling, beaming even. She leant over the cradle and I heard her speaking in her dear voice – a voice that I could not describe but that I would be able to recognize in a million until my dying day – that sing-song voice she had used with me when I was little. Those same intonations, which had welcomed me twenty-five years earlier, chimed again for Mathilde.

I had long hair at the time, all the way down my back. It was so tangled with sweat that it seemed nothing could be done with it. I sat on the bed and handed a comb to my mother, and she undertook to comb my hair. It took a long time. How long was it since the last time she had done that? I was her little girl once again because I was a mother like her. I had a daughter, I was hers. Suddenly we were both young mothers, she and I.

Laurent and I were very carefree. In hospital he would sit cross-legged on my bed and play poker with me. When we left we paid for my stay in hospital at the cashdesk (we had just got back from the United States and Laurent was not yet working), and we forgot the baby at the desk . . .

Between that time and the day that I told you about in my last letter seven years, six months and ten days elapsed. I could happily tell you about Elise's birth too. You know how much women like talking about this sort of thing even though they know no-one is interested! My Elise, my little Elise, I will not tell you anything about her. Except to say that a friend, studying the photograph taken the day before she died – the school photograph in which she appears, sitting cross-legged on the floor in her little sailor collar dress, in the first row on the left – this friend delved into her dark eyes under the long brown fringe, and said quietly: 'It's you. It's just a small version of you.'

Dying young. Dying beautiful. Dying when you are still at nursery school. Dying at four and a half. Dying.

Elise is no longer a smaller version of me, but a bigger one.

30 January 1992

You ou told me yesterday that you were shattered to discover from my last letter that I should now be the mother of a nineteen year-old girl. We were at the café near the Porte de Saint-Cloud, and you were looking at me from behind your glasses from the other side of the square table. I felt myself age ten years. As if your eyes were filming an accelerated process of ten years of withering while you accommodated this revelation. Would we be friends, you and I, if I had a nineteen year-old daughter, my nineteen year-old daughter, and a sixteen year-old daughter, my sixteen year-old daughter? You did not say it but I could hear you thinking:

'You could be a grandmother soon.' Your own son is eleven and a half. I was suddenly older than you, there, in that café. I feel cold. I cannot change any of this. On the 30th of April 1980, a volcano spilt its ashes on us, when I was thirty-three and Laurent thirty-two. The children died, and for us time stood still; it is this stagnation that I am telling you about.

There are other people for whom time passes differently. Those devoted to God, for example. Who can tell the age of a monk or a nun?

I am as old as I am, and I am not. I am not the

mother of those grown-up girls. I do not want to have
both lost my children, and to appear as old as if they had
grown up. I would like you to think of me as you did
before, the mother of children younger than your own.
Yes, they do make me younger. You will have to take all
these complications on board. The realities of one
motherhood are no stronger than the realities of another.
My children are still young, and their older sisters are not
here to baby-sit them or to make me older than I appear.
My age is certainly greater than yours. In any event,
during the course of the days that I was telling you about,
the three days which separated the Wednesday on which
they died and the Saturday on which we held the funeral,
three centuries went by. I can only repeat: the mystery is
impenetrable and I will only deepen it when I tell you
what happened next, if I resolve to do so. Have
confidence in me, and be prepared not to understand
anything. I am afraid that I will never emerge from these
archaeological excavations, that I will bury myself, that I
will disappear before your very eyes.

I promised myself that I would not digress at all, and I
have already broken that promise. You yourself told me
that you could only take this account in small doses. But
this same account – which is pitifully dilute in
comparison with the reality – was the only thing which
kept us going for years.

And another thing. I do not like talking about myself.
All this misfortune happened to them, and only them.
And yet I am talking about myself. I am standing centre-
stage. We will never know anything about them.

12 February 1992

These letters have brought my daughters back into
my life and my dreams, and it seemed unfair to tear
myself away from the sweetness of this rediscovery to
concentrate on their end: hence the silence of the last few
days. Since the death of the girls I often worry whether I
am fair to myself.

I do not even know exactly where I got to. Never
mind. It must have been somewhere on that morning on
which people gradually let each other know, when those
closest to us came over, threw themselves into the street
to make their way to this unknown address in the Avenue
Théophile-Gautier. I can see these shadows, see myself
on the sofa. You know, childhood friends are very useful.
And brothers and sisters. Or more distant friends who,
terrified of failing, nevertheless feel that they have a role
to play. They were all there, whispering in the corridors,
trying to find the best solution. One urgent question kept
presenting itself: where to put us? Where would it be best
for us to suffer?

Catherine, my godfather's daughter, sat next to me and
said something that I did not understand, that I still do
not understand today. But at that moment I knew that in
the mystery and truth of her affirmation there was great

vision. She said: 'They did have a full life all the same.' I
know that one day, before I die, I will understand this
sentence. I know that it is above reason and that in order
to assimilate it I will have to reach a dimension which is
not yet part of me. I know that in a sense, yes, at seven
and a half and four and a half Mathilde and Elise came
onto this earth to perform their human function, a
complete function lacking not one nuance or a single
millimetre of depth. I also know that – because I still feel
so utterly that I am their mother – I can only fiercely
reject that sort of idea and I have to be satisfied with a
feeling of rage at seeing my children robbed of
everything, while in my heart a strange creature still roars
and chafes, an all-powerful chimera which still wants to
save them.

We left and went to stay with Philippe and Françoise,
Laurent's brother and his wife. They had sent their three
little boys to Françoise's mother and had given us their
room. The same day a few friends came over there, near
the Place de la Nation, to lend a hand. Making some
soup, I remember that. Bringing us some clothes too
perhaps? I no longer remember. I started being sick, and
Françoise called the emergency service. A young
psychiatrist came. He worked in the same area of
psychiatry that I had once, we spoke of a hospital in
which I had spent three years of my career and which he
knew well. As he referred to the 'workings of mourning',
I asked him how long it lasted, but he did not know,
poor man. He left a prescription.

There. Thursday evening. The girls had been dead
twenty-four hours. I think that the funeral had already

been mentioned; I had said that I would not go. With
hindsight, it seems impossible to explain this decision. I
can only say that just twenty-four hours after such a
sudden, complete and definitive event, I simply did not
feel concerned with the funeral of the two children who,
only the day before, had been watching a televised
ceremony attended by the grandparents they were going
to see later.

For the same reason, to spare us the pain, an
announcement had been prepared without our
participation and sent to *Le Monde* and *Le Figaro*. On
Friday morning, Aline read the text to me on the
telephone. A long list of people informed the population
of the death of two little girls whose names – coming at
the end of all this – seemed insignificant. My sister had
been missed out of this august procession. I felt myself
re-emerging as wild, autocratic and impermeable to the
practical considerations, and I laughed bitterly when I was
told that it was too late to do anything to change the text
of the obituary announcement. If two little girls could be
killed, then the presses could be stopped, an edition of a
daily paper could be pulped, the head office of *Le Monde*
and *Le Figaro* could even be blown up. Mathilde and
Elise had to be the stars of this announcement. And
those who learned about their death should know the
circumstances. And that is how, after a mad dash across
Paris which I imagined but about which I knew nothing,
the following text was published: 'Laurent and Geneviève
Jurgensen have great pain in announcing the death of
their two little daughters, Mathilde who was seven and a
half, and Elise who was four and a half. They were killed

instantly in a road accident on 30 April 1980.' Followed
by the names of the families involved and the first names
of the cousins.

That same day, Jacques Schneider, the priest who had
baptized the girls, read in the News in Brief section of a
paper he never normally read a short article which
mentioned the accident. He searched through the
archives. Rang our apartment where there was no reply.
Rang Mathilde's godfather who confirmed that it was
indeed about her and her little sister. Jacques Schneider
let us know that he would take communion at the funeral
mass. Jacques Schneider? With him I would go to the
funeral. From one baptism comes another . . . There. I
was there.

undated letter

T· hat Friday morning the doorbell rang and I heard, recognized Raymond's voice asking for me. I went over to him and he said very quietly: 'There are so many people here, do you want me to take you somewhere for a while?' I grabbed my coat and walked along next to him, like a child, holding his hand, to a little café in the Place de la Nation. I talked to him. I held onto his gaze as I often did. I hooked my eyes onto his. His affectionate ironic face. The well-honed remarks with which he used to tease this little girl who was overly serious, assiduous, and trembled at the thought of displeasing him. His company was always episodic, always important. In the past – yesterday – he would come round and in the peace of the apartment we would write songs and screenplays. In the past – the day before yesterday – we were in the same philosophy class together. In the past once he lent me some money because I was in a tight corner, it was a question of life and death. And who, at twenty, has both money and friendship? In the past, on my wedding day, the newspapers talked of his beloved stepfather, a famous politician, who was lost at sea the same day.

I was with Raymond at the café just like in the past. One day – yesterday – he had arrived at the apartment

when I had just gone out to buy some bread for lunch.
When I got back, Mathilde, in a blue and green kilt, was
explaining to him that I would not be long. You will not
find her there any longer, Raymond. Nor her little sister.
They are not there any longer.

My sister had arrived from Savoie, with my brother-in-
law and their son Nicholas. My sister and I had chanted
to each other on the telephone: 'Both of them, both of
them.' I can hear myself telling her: 'both of them,
Christine, they are both dead,' and she replied: 'yes, yes,
both of them.' We had interlaced our voices as in
Pergolesi's *Stabat Mater* which Jacques, her husband, had
gone to buy because I wanted to hear it in church the
next day.

In the evening, sleeping pills. In the morning, we have
to go. We get dressed in the black clothes lent to us by
various people; I particularly remember a cape from my
godmother. I do my hair. Françoise catches me putting
black eye pencil on: 'It's not a good idea,' she says gently.

I do not remember who took us there. I have no
recollection of the journey to Compiègne, where the
service was to be held, followed by the burial in the tomb
where our daughters had recently buried their paternal
great-grandparents. The previous Saturday we had made
the same journey in our 304. Laurent driving, me next to
him, the girls in the back. The house at Compiègne is at
the end of the same road as the church and the cemetery.
It's the same route. Last week, last weekend, we looked
for daffodils in the woods, and Laurent had told us with
his poignant nostalgia how much they had changed, these
woods that reminded him of his childhood, where wild

daffodils and hyacinths grew in a thick carpet of yellow
and blue. Last weekend, Mathilde and Elise had –
goodness only knows why – buried two little identical
dolls in the garden.

It was the same route. I do not remember anything.

25 February 1992

*W*hen I was talking to you yesterday I was thinking
how annoying I must be because I am always trying to
explain myself. Since the girls died, about 140,000 people
have died the same death. On the road. I am always
there, making sure from your expression and your tone of
voice that you are seeing it all, grasping it, getting the
idea. I ask you on the telephone: 'Have you had my
letter?' I remember seven years ago having lunch with
Gabriel Matzneff*. During the conversation, which was
on a completely different subject, I slipped in a remark
about the girls. We were in an Italian restaurant. When,
after a moment of silence, I lifted my eyes from my plate
of carpaccio to meet his beautiful, pale eyes, he was
crying. I can remember how it squeezed my heart, just as
I once used to squeeze those little hands in mine. My
daughters. It was all three of us who had made Gabriel
cry.

So, we arrived at the church square in Compiègne. A
cobbled square. There were silhouettes, many of them,
making their way towards the large doors. I recognize

---

* A famous (and scandalous) French writer.

them, I run over to one, to another, we hug each other. I
say to them: 'I've seen so-and-so arrive, he's already in
the church, go and sit next to him.' There are people
from all walks of life. I want them to be gathered
together, to warm each other up. There are friends from
work, the janitor from our building with the plumber,
there are neighbours, parents of school friends, our
paediatrician, family, cousins from Savoie, the Bertrand
cousins, those from Pierrefonds, my mother's friends, the
successive nannies, the godfathers, the godmothers, those
who looked after me as a child, and those who looked
after Laurent as a child, there was everything that makes
up a life. Flowers, banners with loving messages. I watch
this fabric of people on the pavement most of whom have
never met each other before. And suddenly the little
hearse arrives and I find myself saying: 'Here they are.' I
go ahead of them with Laurent. Some men get the two
coffins out, they are both very small, one even smaller
than the other. I have never seen such small coffins. We
check the inscriptions. There are no mistakes. All that is
left to them is there: their first names, their middle
names, their family name, their birth dates, the date of
their death. The same day for both of them. I gave
Mathilde her name thinking of the proud young woman
loved by Julien Sorel.* Her second name was Marie,
dedicating her to the Holy Virgin. Laurent had named
Elise that she might inspire, as Beethoven had been

---

* The young man at the centre of Stendhal's novel *The Scarlet and the
Black*.

inspired, the most beautiful love-letters, the most
beautiful works of art. And Sarah as her second name
because life is long, hope infinite and motherhood a
triumph. All these beautiful stories were carved into the
copper plates on the blond wood of the coffins. Where
are they now, their Julien Sorels and their Beethovens,
who do not even know what they have missed? Where
are Mathilde and Elise's lovers? Who are they as, even
now, they lean tenderly over someone else's face? 'I might
have married them off to a couple of pretentious young
idiots,' Laurent said a few days later. Hardly. He did not
believe it himself. They would have seduced the masters
of the universe.

We went into the church after our children, followed
them the length of the nave. Two very frail forms
followed us, my mother and my sister-in-law Aline. The
pretty young aunt who had been driving the car. The
young mother — where was her baby? I did not know
who was looking after Aude that day — Aline who was
thirteen when I met her brother. She had given us her
dog's stud fees to pay for our honeymoon! She was so
young, she would always be the little sister — whom
Laurent would never call anything but 'sweetie' — she got
married and asked her nieces to be bridesmaids, she had a
baby quickly to be like the others, and she set off like
that on her adult life, driving the car from which the two
little bridesmaids would be ejected.

3 March 1992

*D*o you know the Brassens song about the little
horse, 'Wasn't He Brave'? 'He was killed in a flash of
light, all behind, all behind, all behind, and him in front.'
That was it. Our girls were so brave, with us behind and
them out in front. We were just following. There was
both a tender atmosphere of childhood – with all the
flowers, their nicknames on the banners, the sweet-peas,
the ribbons, the sailor dresses and the patent leather
shoes that I had wanted them to wear – and a feeling of
the end of life, the path to infinity which had been
trodden by all four of my grandparents and my father.
We were processing up the nave out of order: us behind,
them in front.

A madwoman was blocking the entrance of the church.
She was dressed in *moiré* fabric, in some grotesque sort of
medieval costume, and she was screaming angrily. I could
not tell you exactly what she was saying, it was something
to do with butchery, carnage. She was making a lot of
noise. I said to Laurent: 'She can't stay here,' and Laurent
said that the church is open to everyone. He was right.
She yelled through the whole ceremony, but I hardly
heard her. I learned later that my cousin Pierre could not
stand it, that he suffered on my account and said to my

aunt: 'this is unbearable for Vève,' but did not want to get involved, afraid that that would only cause more of a fuss. As for Françoise she had imagined that, as the mad woman seemed to be some sort of mystic, she had told her that the Pope was waiting for her outside the town hall . . .

The mass. Sobs wash over me in a swell which, as I remember it, keep me standing. But Laurent remembers having to come to my aid. The communion. My sister passes in front of me, I feel her hands in my hair, she buries her face in it and says: 'Nico has just communicated for the first time.' Have I already mentioned Nico to you? My nephew, the only child of my blood alive on that day. He was eight. The family no longer existed and would no longer exist in his generation. In the crowd, amongst other children are Dorothée and Fabienne, the 'twin sisters' of my daughters. At the beginning of the school year when Dorothée's mother saw that she was not in the same class as Mathilde she broke down. And when Mathilde used to go to the nursery to pick Elise up, the teacher would often get confused and call Fabienne, or conversely, she would call Elise if it was Dorothée who came to the classroom door. There they were, Dorothée and Fabienne, to bury their doubles.

I learned later that Françoise had said to Tristan, Mathilde's beloved cousin: 'No-one will ever love you as she did.'

We received condolences. I wanted to see people one at a time. I wanted to see this procession of helpful people who were there, present, loved before, loved during, loved tomorrow. I wanted to see them, to tell

them clearly how effective their presence was. I wanted a
queen's burial for my daughters: I got it.

Then we went on to the cemetery. Family, a few
friends. It was a beautiful day. The grave-diggers had
asked whether we wanted the children to be put into the
tomb one on top of the other or head to foot: they could
only be put next to each other if they were head to foot.
That's the solution we adopted. There were birds singing
and Laurent's grandmother said, with her Burgundy
accent: 'Of course they're singing, they're at peace here.'

It was over. All we had left to do was to get home.
Françoise had made a meal. In the afternoon I went over
to my mother to see my aunt and uncle who would soon
be returning to Haute-Savoie. The concierge came out of
her lodge to see me as I went into the building. Mathilde
often used to go over to play with her daughter. She said:
'you will see, you can get used to anything.' It is certainly
the most simple, true, brutal and perceptive thing that
anyone said to me at the time. You could interpret it
either as a message of hope or of crushing contempt for
human nature.

I have now finished telling you about the three days
that separated life with my daughters from life without
them. Up till now it has seemed easy. But the rest . . . It
cannot be chronological, my memory would not allow it.
I would probably have to go back to my diaries of that
period. I would find arrangements made innocently for
my daughters after the 30th of April. Dental
appointments, birthday parties. The time of the flight on
which I had reserved seats for them for 'Holland', as
Mathilde called it. How do you expect me to do that?

13 March 1992

*W*hy have I not written to you for so long? Just now
I felt like ringing you and inviting you to Sunday lunch
with friends in a couple of weeks' time, but I resisted the
urge, because I thought that if I speak to you I will not
write to you.

On the Monday I went to the dentist in Mathilde's
place. I had made the appointment for her and it struck
me that it would be easier to honour it than to cancel it.
Having to say: 'Would you apologize to the dentist for
my daughter, she won't be able to come because she is
dead' did not appeal to me. Did my mother go with me?
It is very likely that she did. The dentist, who has been
my dentist since my childhood, watched with
consternation as I got into the chair: 'You shouldn't have
come, Mrs Jurgensen,' he said. I knew that he had lost an
older brother, that made things easier. Laurent had gone
back to work. He was silent, nauseous and often tearful.
That was out of the question for me: as a speech
therapist, I worked only with children. A friend of Aline's
helped me to warn off the parents of those who came
to my own consulting-room (which was the dining-
room!) and at the Alfred Binet Centre friends had made
sure that parents knew they should wait until further

notice. One evening at the beginning of that week – I
am no longer sure which day it was – we had to leave
Françoise and Philippe's apartment near the Place
de la Nation. My parents-in-law had gone back to the
Hague, we could go to their apartment which was in a
big block overlooking the Seine. Philippe and Françoise
had to go and pick up their three sons, who were still
with their grandmother in Palaiseau, while a solution was
being found for us. We packed up our little bags. It
began to feel like an exile, as if we were a couple of
strays. Laurent's grandmother, Minnie, left her villa in
Mâcon with its garden in all its spring glory to come and
keep an eye on us. I think she was eighty-four years old.
I loved her. She was ashamed to be alive still. When we
arrived in the Rue Emeriau, supper was ready, there were
tons of mail waiting for us and a few members of the
family stood arm in arm, forming a gallant but shaky
reception committee. Laurent would have preferred to go
home.

Letters of condolence. If a friend of yours loses
someone, write them a letter full of love. You need them,
these letters, to help get you through the days and the
evenings somehow. You open them, you read, you search
through them for the *mot juste*, and you always find it.
However distant the author of the letter may be, he is
there, vigilant; he helps you to look at your life; he says
that he knows, that he is thinking, that he will keep and
protect. The letters cement the bricks laid down by the
survivors. Write, write, write. Do not miss one
opportunity to do it. If you have the choice between
writing and not writing, always choose to write. Not a

single letter is out of place. We had letters from people
who had heard us mentioned by mutual friends, people
we had never met. Everything is a help. Each of us can
be of help to everyone else. I have kept all of these letters
and of course I have never reread them. I have forgotten
the words. Superhuman efforts to reach us through the
inadequacies of language are enclosed in great extending
envelopes. Were these efforts made in vain? Of course
they were not. You should have seen me waiting for the
post, opening the envelopes, reading feverishly,
commenting, storing away. Then going on to dream
about what had been written. Lending it the full weight
of my distress. The letters paved the path between my
daughters and myself. I was a letter-ogre. I hungered for
them, each one satisfied me until the next one arrived.
You have no idea of the state of delirium into which this
sort of torture can plunge you. Mathilde had a little
friend who appears next to her in the class photograph.
This friend had a guinea pig which had just had babies.
Mathilde wanted us to have one of them. I was not
against the idea but, as we had just lost our dog, I asked
her to wait a while, to give us time to get over the loss of
Triton (loss is exactly the word: he just disappeared on
the streets). So Mathilde died before the end of this
period of mourning that I had wanted her to respect.
Probably out of shyness, that little girl's mother never got
in touch with me. She lives three houses from us: several
times I was just in front of her or behind her at the
grocer's shop, and she never said hello. Can you believe
that for months I thought her silence meant she was
happy that my daughter had died because she had been a

bad influence on her daughter. There is absolutely no
doubt that silence is open to the bleakest of
interpretations. You have to come out of the woods
into the open and say: I am here, I know, I have seen,
I am witnessing, I am here. If you stay in the woods
you are saying just as clearly: I am not here, I know
nothing, I have seen nothing, I am turning my back on
you.

On the subject of Triton, our dog, here is a little
anecdote: Laurent and I adopted him in Chicago where
we were studying. Therefore, before the girls were born.
He was a beagle, a little pack dog; he was unpredictable,
a runaway and charming. We no longer kept count of the
number of times he had run away, nor the times that he
had come home in the middle of the night, encrusted
with dirt, and barking at the door for his food. Just as
often we had to go and pick him up from the police
station. Usually he would piece together his pack of local
dogs, who were quite well behaved, and lead them all
over town, goodness knows where. And then one evening
he really did not come home.

We searched the kennels of the SPA and the dog
pounds without success. Mathilde cried but Elise, who
was determined to be in control of the situation, said: 'we
must throw away his lead now, we don't need it any
more.'

Nonetheless, I put up little posters with a photograph
of my dog in the local shops. One of the photographs –
it was at the bakery in the Rue de La Fontaine – was of
Mathilde in a blue coat with a hood, holding Triton. I
avoided going to that bakery for years. I neither wanted

to see her again, nor to see that she had been taken down from the window. But, more than that, the subject of the 'missing' notice had changed, you see.

13 March 1992

$\mathcal{I}$t was at that time that we went back to the school to speak to the children's teachers. Elise's teachers told us that at break time Elise often preferred to stay inside with Fabienne: they would both take sponges and carefully clean the little tables. Mathilde's class mistress liked to think of a children's tea party a few weeks earlier to which she had been invited, and where Mathilde had asked her to dance. I know that a service in memory of these two pupils was held in the school chapel, but we were not living at home when the mother superior came round to let us know and the message never got to us. I think that there is not one child in Elise's class who can remember her today. Those children in the 'pink playschool' are now sixteen years old. But in Mathilde's class, the C.E. 1, there are some who could tell us something: a story, an image, an impression. Years later on the *métro* I met the mother of Andrea, a little girl who had invited Elise to her fourth birthday party. She told me that she had photographs of the afternoon. And so I saw my younger daughter as I had never seen her before, playing follow my leader with other little girls, looking into the lens over the shoulder of the child in front. I looked at the clothes I had dressed her in that

day. I really liked Andrea's mother. She was a stranger
with a gentle central European face. She reminded me of
Unesco, a *milieu* that my father liked to live in. It made
me happy to think that one Wednesday afternoon while I
was working she had watched over my Elise as she
played. I could imagine her impotent sorrow when the
photographs were developed and a part of that little
world was already dead.

20 March 1992

I had a quick cup of coffee with a journalist this
morning. He arrived with his daughter who had slept
badly and was going to spend the day in her father's
office. She was dressed in a spring dress with navy blue
sandals and an Austrian jacket; she rummaged in her
father's pockets to empty out their contents, twiddled
with her white cuddly kitten and skipped about excitedly
on the paving stones. From the other side of the table I
watched what I had lost almost twelve years earlier, but it
was still a happy moment.

In the stream of mail that I was talking about there
was a card which announced: 'Hurray, Raphaël has
arrived!' It obviously came as a surprise in amongst these
letters of condolence. Our friends the Ns were
announcing the arrival of their second son, not realizing
that we did not have any children any longer. What
should we do? How could we congratulate and inform in
the same breath? How could we give such appalling news
to childhood friends whose family had just increased? I
decided first of all to give them a present for the baby,
and to let them know or make sure they were told later.
Nathalie took me to see Dominique, my godfather's
second daughter, who had opened a baby clothes shop in

the Rue de la Tour. Dominique had lost her two year-old
son; he had been drowned in a swimming pool some time
before. Nathalie was pregnant. What a time it was!

At the shop I could feel that Nathalie could barely
contain herself. She wanted us to leave, she regretted
letting herself be talked into it. 'Come on, Vève, we're
going,' she said. What on earth was I doing there, I who
had buried my daughters the week before? My hands on
the fresh cotton fabrics, looking at the price tickets and
comparing the sizes . . . I ended up choosing something,
slipped a little note – 'with hugs and kisses' – into the
parcel, and we dropped it off at the Ns', on the landing
or with the concierge, I do not remember. Forty-eight
hours later Nathalie rang them to tell them who this
present really came from. The last time I had seen
Catherine N was in the street not far from our
apartment. A chance encounter when I had gone to pick
Mathilde up at the end of a dancing class. Elise was there
too. Catherine will never see me at the dancing class with
my girls again. I always felt as if I had committed some
offence when I told them this harsh truth, which could
only waken a terrifying echo in them.

We had to go back to the apartment to sort out the
girls' clothes and belongings. That is what Nathalie and I
did.

I am thinking about that little girl again, the one I saw
this morning at the café with her father. Spring dress,
navy blue sandals, Austrian jacket and fluffy white kitten.
A list which immediately evokes another: beads, crayons,
records, an apple. Vests and underpants from Petit
Bateau. Navy blue uniforms. Gym clothes, winter

pyjamas, summer night-dresses. Toothbrushes, fruit-flavoured toothpaste. Roller-skates, Play-Doh, little bamboo chair, Fisher Price dolls' house. Mickey sheets, musical bedside light.

Nathalie brought three big metal trunks. She watched over me. She said stop. She took me back to my in-laws' apartment. She said she would see me the next day.

14 April 1992

I have not written to you for a long time. Since we
went to the mountains? I do not know. If I really have
not written to you since then, a whole month has gone
by.

It is very strange, this double rhythm that I have with
you. I write to you, forcing myself to clarify a period of
my life that I have done everything I can to understand, a
period which I have tried to allow to pervade me rather
than defending myself from it, but which has always been
out of my grasp. It is said that reality outstrips fiction;
but this is something else. The reality remains
inaccessible. I know that I have always dreamed my life
and that my dreams have been my most stark reality. But
since the death of the girls – twelve years in sixteen days'
time – I have honestly and constantly tried to unveil this
reality without success. Perhaps I have already told you:
sometimes I believe in them alive (my darling children,
my darling little girls; these words which are so light and
yet so burdensome cut through me then), and sometimes
I believe in their death (on the edge of the motorway, ten
or so metres from each other; their legs in dungarees,
their arms and heads on the side of the motorway). There
is never a link between the two.

The other rhythm constitutes the things I do in my
current life as if nothing had happened. Conversations,
laughter, mutual friends. A double rhythm like a double
life: you do not know whether they struggle against each
other or enrich each other.

I had some real excuses for not writing to you. A
(provisional) change of job after thirteen months of
waiting and the election of the regional committee. But
above all I was busy living my life, my life now. Having a
rest.

Have I already mentioned Yasser Arafat to you? This is
what made me think of him: when Elise was born, I
found myself battling with a huge hungry baby. The few
odd ounces of milk that I was able to supply in the first
twenty-four hours of her life in hospital were definitely
not enough for her and she screamed constantly. With
Mathilde crying down the telephone because she felt lost
without me, I quickly lost my patience. I found myself
brutally grasping Elise's cradle, which was on casters, and
furiously pushing it away from my bed so that it was in
danger of banging into the far wall. A second of silence
and the crying started up again. On the third day my
mother came to see me: she had left Mathilde with Aline
for a few hours, just long enough to come and see her
second granddaughter. She came with Samy, with whom
she had more or less been living since my father had
died. They sat at the end of the bed and chatted; we were
cheerful. Elise, who had just suckled, was curled up on
my lap, pressed against my legs which were drawn up
under the sheets. We, the adults, were talking to each
other, but I was looking at my daughter who was looking

back at me. Drawn by her gaze, I leant over her and
rubbed my nose on hers. She said 'huh, huh'. I stared at
my mother to reassure myself that I had not dreamed it.
It had quite knocked the breath out of her. I did the
same thing again and Elise replied again. Third attempt,
third exchange. And that was it, she was my child, my
treasure, my stupefaction. The next day I signed my own
discharge to the annoyance of the doctor so that I could
take her home, despite her rather doubtful chest X-rays. I
was in no doubt. I never doubted in her or myself again.

For logistical reasons it was my mother who came with
Mathilde to pick me up from hospital. I went down one
of the big staircases. At the end of one of the ground-
floor corridors I saw Mathilde in her little green loden
coat; she was watching silently, motionless, her nose
pointing up another staircase. My mother pointed me out
to her and Mathilde started to walk towards me slowly. I
handed Elise to my mother so that I could lift Mathilde
into her rightful place in my arms. I can still feel to the
nearest ounce the pressure of her legs around my waist.
She did not say anything but she slowly and silently felt
my face with her hands like a blind girl. During this
rediscovery, this tender and cautious reunion, my mother
was smiling and whispering sweet nothings to Elise. She
had brown hair, olive skin and huge eyes ringed with
black kohl, and – to confront the October weather – she
was wearing a woollen hat which was a bit too big for
her which skewed sideways over her ear. 'She could be
Yasser Arafat's daughter!' my mother laughed.

The other day, the radio announced that Yasser
Arafat's plane had disappeared in a sandstorm in the

Libyan desert. A few hours later, although the members of his entourage were killed or injured, he himself was found alive and grinning.

Every time that a tragic event affects him but spares him – the murder of an adviser, all sorts of attempts on his life or an aeroplane crash – I feel that hug again. When I think of the life he leads and the life that Elise led, when I think of the life expectancy they each had on that October day when my mother teased me about my daughter – to think that she is dead and he is here.

30 April 1992

*W*ell, it is twelve years now. On Sunday we went to
the grave. The journey to Compiègne was also their last
journey; dead or alive they have never left Picardy since
the afternoon of Beatrix's coronation. In the cemetery we
put down the rosebushes and thoroughly cleaned the
collection of seashells gathered for them by the children
in the family. On the headstone there are some cherubs:
they are not meant to represent them or watch over them
but to point out to passers-by that this is a children's
grave. Next to where their names are carved in the stone
there is the head of a chubby little angel with its wings
spread. We had their names engraved separately:
'Mathilde Marie Jurgensen, 20 October 1972, 30 April
1980 – Elise Sarah Jurgensen, 8 October 1975, 30 April
1980.' An angel next to Mathilde, an angel next to Elise.
Whenever people come to see them, the last person there
changes the little prop fixed behind the wings of each
angel, taking a stick from one of the trees planted at the
corners of the grave. Two very different trees, which
shocks some people but then our daughters were very
different. Two distinct people in two distinct coffins are
buried there. So one of the trees is growing well and the
other has not grown at all, and that is just the way it is.

We really like going to the grave, tidying it up, gardening, cleaning it rather as we used to in their room in the evening, before the last kiss, before having long talks with them in the dark, we would fold up their things, get their shoes together, close the drawers and the cupboard doors. Laurent would often pretend to butter their plump little feet and bite into them.

But at the same time I feel drained at their graveside. Just as, immediately after their death, I could not wait to join them, I wanted to open the grave as you would a book and to slip into it as if between sheets to be with them again, to close my eyes and give back the thirty-three year-old mother to my girls of seven and four; now it does not do anything for me any more to keep going to Compiègne, to that cemetery surrounded by cheap flats, to be with these girls who would not recognize me if they saw me, girls who should now be doing university entrance exams – in the case of the younger one – and getting married – for the older one.

Gauthier likes digging round the grave, supposedly to help dig in the pots so that the wind does not blow them over. In fact I think he hopes he will see his sisters. This Sunday he said: 'You're lucky, you know everything about my sisters, and I don't know anything.' Yes, that is it. We know everything, we will never know any more. And he will never know anything of them.

When we left the cemetery we went towards the forest. The forest in Compiègne has always made me uneasy, besides I have always felt excluded, locked out . . . it holds too many memories for Laurent which are not associated with me.

The telephone rings, the children wake up, I have to
get breakfast, and the efforts that I make to reach you
and to reach Mathilde and Elise are thwarted by the
efforts I must make in my everyday life.

I am trying to explain to you that twelve years and one
week ago, we were coming home from Compiègne with
the girls, that Laurent was talking about the daffodils of
his childhood, and the little ones were singing in the back
of the car. What is more I think it was that evening that
I tartly asked Mathilde to be quiet because she was
singing off-key and, turning to look at her, I saw her face
drop and I felt guilty.

We were to make the trip back six days later, without
our daughters, whom we were to find on the square in
front of Saint-Jacques and to bury.

Right, now I will stop. I will do what I have to do for
the living and then I will come back to you because I
have masses of things to tell you.

Sunday, then. I have come back to last Sunday. We
left the cemetery, put the gardening things in the car and
made our way to the woods so that Gauthier could do
some bicycling. We parked the car and took the bicycle
out. There is no-one on the track except for a couple
with a baby, strolling thoughtfully. Gauthier gets onto his
bicycle. I slip my handbag under the carseat so that it will
not get in the way as I run behind my son. Laurent and I
are talking about something or other. I notice that at
eight Gauthier still has not progressed from braking with
his feet and I think of the son of some friends who is the
same age. I say to myself: 'I'm sure he already knows how
to use his brake levers.' We go all the way back along the

track, in the end I do not have to run, the atmosphere is
conducive to strolling, but after visiting the cemetery I
would have preferred not to stroll, I would have liked to
run so that I could not think. Gauthier returned to the
car with us. Did he really open the door that I had
definitely locked with Laurent's keys? Yes, he opened it.
Yes, it had been forced. Yes, my handbag had been
stolen.

'They' had: my keys, along with my identity papers
which gave our address; my cheque book, with examples
of my signature on the identity papers; my credit cards,
my travel pass, my sports club card, my professional card;
my pass for the canteen; my whole diary with a scramble
of appointments right through to September; my address
book, with eight years of precious addresses gathered in
years of meetings; medical prescriptions, favourite
photographs of favourite people, including one of myself
in jeans coiled up with Mathilde, teaching her to read, in
the depths of a big armchair. They have Gauthier's
identity card, the papers for the car, 800 francs in cash,
my toothbrush, my pens and pencils, my comb, my
telephone card, my near-sighted glasses. You know, they
have my things. A little twist of a screw-driver in the
lock and ciao.

Gauthier wants an ice-cream. As his sisters once did,
he likes to buy ice-creams in the woods from pedlars. I
persuade myself that nothing is that serious, the sisters
are dead, we are not going to make a song and dance
about a little annoyance. Destination: the police station.
While I am explaining what has happened Laurent rings
the emergency numbers for stopping cheques and credit

cards. The police officer asks me the car registration
number. Without hesitating I say: '729 BCD 75.' I do
not hesitate but I feel strange. He senses my uneasiness
and asks: 'Are you sure?' What does he think! I know
the number of my car! He is not convinced. He gets up
and types the number out onto a screen. He draws a
blank, it says that the car does not belong to me, I
cannot think what it means, and anyway Laurent is
coming back over so I get up and glance at our car
parked outside the police station. A solid Volvo, bought
when Elvire was born eleven years earlier, in which
perhaps that baby would survive. I look at the number
plate: 228 DPH 75.

I had given the police the previous number, the 304,
the girls' car. We had broken the cylinder head gasket a
few days before they were to leave for Holland. So that
when Aline and Christian asked if they could borrow it
to take everyone there, with its new engine block the 304
was still being run in and would really have held them up
too much on their journey. Hence the Renault 5, hence
death. One of the cogs of death. And, standing there in
this police station, I do not want any of this. Not the
broken gasket, nor the dead children, or the stolen bag,
not this life which keeps slipping out of my fingers, the
more you struggle to get up the hill, the more it smacks
you on the head and forces you to go down, further
down, even further. 729 BCD 75. There lies the truth. It
all comes down to that.

We get back to Paris. We have to call the locksmith,
and change everything straight away. It is such a pleasure
signing cheques at times like this: it is so good to have a

problem which can be resolved with money! The next
morning I have had a night filled with bad dreams.
(Elvire is in Normandy with a friend, as in real life. As in
real life, I cannot get hold of her, I only made a note of
the address and telephone number in my diary which has
been stolen. In my dream she speaks to me about
Normandy, I can see her but I cannot answer, but she
looks pale and she gradually fades away despite my best
efforts, she tells me she is dead and I try to call her as
the daffodils thrust into my mouth, their roots down my
throat, I call her but the sounds do not come out. I wake
groaning and try to reassure myself. Elvire, Gauthier,
Mathilde, Elise, half of my children, which half of my
children, it is time to get up, but I go back to sleep in a
state of fear.) I go to work at the paper at eight o'clock. I
have hardly been there five minutes when an incident
erupts over a week-old article of mine about Arte being
featured regularly on the fifth channel. Arte? You mean
we have to get upset about Arte? I can feel that my
mouth is open and I cannot close it. I stick myself behind
my computer, type three briefs and go down to my other
office. Is Philippe (the artistic director I usually work
with) there? No. Not this early. The telephone rings, it is
a colleague. And I am crying. Life is so horrible. I pour
my heart out. Oh, it is really horrible.
I can tell he is floundering. But life is horrible!
Horrible! He asks me what I am doing for lunch,
nothing, I cannot be doing anything since I have lost my
diary. I have no more meetings until the end of my days.
I had lunch with him. It takes great strength to catch you
as you spiral away. And great courage too. Especially

from someone who only rang to say hello, but who takes you as you are and manages to bring you gently back to earth.

9 May 1992

$\mathcal{I}$ have some work to hand in, a lot, but nothing will
get done until 1 have written to you. At first it was the
other way around: everything came before writing these
letters. I used to tell myself:

'Why suffer? What's the point of this artificial
rendezvous with these long-lost children?' I always had
something happier to do. Now, even as I get up, I am
carried by the things I want to write to you.

I *should* have gone to see, in that room in the hospital,
where they put my daughters. I knew as soon as they
suggested it to me. I knew that by refusing I was setting
a precedent for a future of weakness because I was not
worthy of . . . I do not know what. Just not worthy. As I
sat on that chair in the office, with my raincoat on, I was
physically incapable of getting to my feet, going through
the door, letting myself be led through the corridors,
entering the room indicated to me, and of going up to
the two bodies – children of seven and a half and four
and half whose hoods I had done up under their chins
that very day to play a practical joke on their
grandmother. Even today, when I have lived nearly three
times longer without them than with them, I would like
to open the drawer in which I kept Elise's underwear,

grab a vest and put it on her. The vest would smell fresh
and the cotton would squeak a little in my hands because
I would not have used a fabric conditioner. I would try to
put her blouse on as quickly as possible – I know that
little shiver over her skin when I have just taken off her
nightie. Her head is so wide that it does not pass easily
through the neck. That little moment when the garment
catches, when you have to tug a bit, is something I did
every day since her birth. October the 8th, 1975, even
then I really had to want to do it to get her head
through. Then, blinded by the clothes, Elise fumbles for
the armholes. I guide her a little. One arm, the other,
there we are. The straps mould to her broad, tanned,
rounded shoulders. I bring the brilliant white fabric down
over her back, her great upright back and her little
tummy. I take this last chance to run the flat of my hand
under the shirt, over her skin. My beautiful child, shall I
put on your dress or your dungarees! Soon she will break
away from me. But at this moment she is my dark-haired
youngest child, there on my knees. She smells of child
and of clean clothes. She is intimidating, there is
something overwhelming in the majesty of this serious
silent little girl. Twelve years later, I still have not
finished taking off Elise's nightclothes and slipping on
her first daytime clothes before she catches cold.

So, I did not go to see them dead. They were there
and Mummy did not come. They were only one or two
rooms away. They remained alone. Mummy did not cross
the doorway. I know nothing of their faces as they were
at the end. They had the strength to die and I could not
match their strength. I know nothing of their last great

achievement. Wherever they went, they went alone.
Together or apart — and I am inclined to believe it was
apart — ignorant of their own heroism, they went to the
places dictated by their violent trajectory at more than
100 km per hour over the safety barrier. I stayed on my
chair like a lump. And since then people have not
stopped congratulating me for my courage as a mother.

To such an extent that many friends, including you,
hesitated before talking to us about the difficulties and
hardships they were facing. They did not seem worthy in
comparison. Laurent and I sat enthroned on a pedestal,
hoisted there by the annihiliation of our two little girls.
But we still knew what real life was, like a weather map
of constantly changing skies, and we needed people to tell
us about it, because the air was thin for our two statues.
The only stance that I battle against is to threaten
suicide. To keep those around you on tenterhooks
because you claim you are going to die. Watch out, I'm
going to kill myself! My goodness, the living can make a
fuss, with their moods, and their other half running all
over the place trying to stop them . . . like cackling
poultry, the cockerel with his crest askew, the chickens
flapping about with their feathers all puffed up, I'm going
to kill myself, watch out, watch out! Oh, no, that is not
how you do it. I will explain to these maniacs how
Mathilde and Elise managed to die. If I can, that is,
because they did the whole thing by themselves, and
when the adults came to their senses and began to realize
that they were no longer in the car, not even under the
front seats where they looked once they realized the rear
seat was empty; when they had to resign themselves to

getting out of the car to look for them – they had to be found, wherever they might be; when it was done, and they had been found, dozens of metres from the car and dozens of metres apart, they had actually already gone, without a word, to a place that no man can see.

All of this brings me back to that moment of weakness on my chair when, even though two children, my two children, two very young children, had known how to die and were waiting to be presented to me one last time in their truthfulness, I had not even gone those few metres along the corridor that separated them from me. They had known how to die, I no longer knew how to walk.

There has been nothing glorious about the way I live my life. I love the living, in all their miasma. I love the dead, for their temerity. There is nothing in between.

13 May 1992

I must get back to the chronology of this account. It
will take a great effort, not because it all seems so long
ago, but because it is against my nature to go backwards.
Someone told me yesterday about a kind of car that has
no reverse gear: I must be built a bit like that. This
month of May is nothing but parties, bank holidays and
departures, the opposite of what I need to write to you.
What is more, I have just remembered you are in
England yourself. I would like even you to stay at home
and not move around! How can I concentrate with all
this coming and going?

Twelve years ago Nathalie came to pick me up in her
car and I went up to the apartment with her to sort
through the children's things. She told me when it was
time to stop. One morning she could not come and she
said that I should not go to my own home by myself. I
went anyway. It was a beautiful day and the children's
fourth floor window was open onto the courtyard. I
did not go into their room, I just glanced at it. I was
wearing a white dress my mother had just bought me,
which made me look good. I made my way to the
dining-room where we kept our stereo and the records. I
knew what I was going to do, nothing could stop me, I

had to do it, I would deal with the effects when I got to
them.

Over the past few weeks Elise had made us go to see
The Jungle Book four times in a cinema near the Porte de
Saint-Cloud which has since disappeared. The first time
all three of us went, Mathilde, Elise and myself. The end
of the film really tormented Elise. Did you take your son
Pierre to see it? Mowgli, urged on by Baloo and
Bagheera, goes back to the man-village. He crosses the
river hesitantly, takes a hold of himself, looks back. It is a
terrible wrench. His 'parents' encourage him. Soon
Mowgli sees a beautiful little girl; she is dark, scantily
clad, on her way to fill her water pot at the river. She is
singing. The words? I remember them: 'I will go to fetch
the water for my home'. It is those two words: 'my
home', sung by a little girl, that I want to hear again. We
had bought the record and Elise listened to it again and
again. I know where it is. I pull it from between the
others with the end of my fingernail, I take the vinyl
from its sleeve, put it on the turntable, bring the arm
across so that the needle is over exactly the right grooves.
She sings, she is going to fetch water for her home. I am
crouching on the floor. From the other side of the
corridor is their luminous room, and at the far end of the
room, the window, the sun. The floor suddenly tips over.
I slip as if the floor is moving beneath me. I find myself
on all fours in the corridor, my nails digging into the
carpet, my limbs spread like buttresses to stop me falling.
Soon I will cross the doorway to their room. It slopes
more and more steeply, I feel very giddy, I can feel it
dragging me sluggishly, drawing me out, I know that I

am going to go through the window. I am carried by it.
The telephone wire trails along the ground, I grab it
between the third and fourth fingers of my left hand and
twist it round my wrist, and there is a noise of heavy
plastic, of a piece of equipment coming apart as it falls:
the telephone, the earpiece, the receiver, it is all spread all
over the floor, but it is working, I can hear the dialling
tone. I dial my mother's number. Answer, Mum, answer.
She is there. She says: 'Come straight away.' She lives at
the end of the street from me. I went straight away. But
when I rang at her door, she opened it, her face ravaged
and haggard, and put arms round me. 'Where have you
been?' she said. 'I've been waiting for over an hour.'

14 May 1992

If I had died that day, everyone would have thought
they understood. Such a natural death! But it would have
been an accidental death. When I put Elise's record on I
had wanted to rediscover the taste of her life. That is
what made me so dizzy. Since then, I have been careful. I
have never watched the films in which my two daughters
appear, nor have I listened to their voices on the
answering machine tapes that my mother kept. The
messages to 'Maminette'* are at her house, accessible, but
I do nothing about it.

How many catastrophes have there been since I began
this correspondence with you? Football stadiums collapse,
young motorbikers kill each other at the 24-hour race in
Le Mans, and here I am with the children and you, and I
tug at my net which is plunged so deep in the water. Last
week I spent a long time looking at a car exactly like the
one in which my daughters fell asleep, from which they
were thrown, in which – leaving their parents to go to
their grandparents – they left Paris never to return. I was
there, looking at the back seat, the seat-belts that we had

---

* *Grannykins, Nannakin*

not done up, the right-hand window out of which they would both have been thrown. The letters on the number plate confirmed it: this Renault 5 was from the same year as my sister-in-law's. They are still on the road, those cars. When there are none left, I will no longer be able to ask questions of them. Someone will have to keep one somewhere for me.

After the impact, when my sister-in-law managed to bring her car to a halt, she and her husband turned with relief to smile at the children. But only their baby was there, sitting in her little seat stupefied, with some fragments of glass spread over her. Have I already told you that? I tell it to myself so many times. When I was near that Renault 5 the other day, I wanted to lie down on the rear seat and wait for the end of time. In short, back to square one.

23 June 1992

Silence is not easily broken. Sometimes, I no longer
understand why I bother you with my daughters' fate.
They spent seven and four years on this earth. What
difference is there to those who spent seventy or forty
years? I am ashamed of everything. Ashamed of these
letters, ashamed of not having saved my daughters' lives,
ashamed of what followed, ashamed of the world which I
have contented myself with since then. Today, for
example, saw the publication of the first issue of the new
magazine, *Interview*. I am adapting to a world which
invests in anything so long as it can 'cough up some
cash', as the saying goes. The grasping expression, the
terrifying mouth and the breasts of the young woman on
the front cover would not trouble me so much if the
balance between the beautiful and the ugly had been
respected a bit more! The death of the girls raised the
threshold of the beautiful too high up on the scale.

I wish I could skip through the account of those
months, those years, four years I think, which followed
the accident. People did what they could. But what could
they do? Is it that that you wanted to know?

I have factual recollections of some episodes without
really understanding how they happened. Ten days

'afterwards', for example, I rang my gynaecologist to stop
my contraception. Laurent and I had said: 'The girls
would have had at least two children each. We should
bring four into the world.' I was thirty-three – it was
possible.

Because we had friends in common, I was convinced
that my gynaecologist knew that my children were dead.
So I called her. But she knew nothing, and in the same
sentence I told her of the end of the older children and
the plans for the next. I heard her trying to catch her
breath on the end of the line. 'Come straight away,' she
managed to say eventually, and I replied coldly that I did
not want anything more than an appointment the
following week whenever there was a gap in her diary.

I would not be able to say when we made love for the
first time. I do not remember it. We probably never
stopped.

I always say 'Mathilde and Elise'. When they were
alive we usually said 'Mathilde' or 'Elise'. Actually, for
three years we had only said 'Mathilde'. Their common
death has made them into siamese twins. Never again will
anyone think of them as two distinct people, as distinct
as my sister and myself.

We wanted other children, then, children to whom we
would be sort of grandparents, as they were to be the
children that Mathilde and Elise would not have
themselves. For her part, when my mother saw
photographs of myself and my sister as children she felt
as if it was us that she had lost. The generations were all
upside down.

In amongst the appalling memories of this period are

my visits to children's clothes shops. I took dresses, T-shirts and jeans from the rails. I looked at the tags, the prices, the sizes. I chatted to the sales girls. Then I would say: 'I will have to come back with my daughters, I can hardly buy anything without them.' And I would find myself back out on the pavement, reeling.

Those who loved us spent a treasure-trove of skill on making the hours go by. My mother got some tickets for us to go and see Montherlant's *Port-Royal* at the Comédie-Française and though, in her own grief, barely able to organize anything, she had even decided to take her car to get us there. In the state she was in it would be quite an achievement to get to that part of the city in the rush-hour, and to park with a daughter and a son-in-law who could barely stand up on their own! We arrived in the square on a mild June evening. After circling several times, my mother spotted a free space and began to manoeuvre the car cautiously. She put the indicator on but, as she started turning her heavy steering wheel, a more sprightly car slipped in front of the parking meter. I got out quickly and leant over the driver's window to explain to him that my mother was just about to park in the place that he had taken. The man was dressed in suit and tie, and he smiled as he cut his engine and jingled his keys gently under my nose, while his wife – in her best clothes and red lipstick – leant over to say: 'Enjoy your evening, my dear!'

My knees shook throughout the play. I did not hear a single word of the text. To this day I harbour for that little couple all the hatred that I do not feel for the boy who killed my children.

22 July 1992

Yesterday I took my children to swim in the rivers of
the Cévennes region. It was perfect. The hillsides, the
trees, the flowers by the side of the cool water, the
current, the pebbles, the fish and even the journey,
particularly the return journey after such a lovely day, in
the old car that we leave here: a Peugeot that my mother
bought the year that Mathilde was born. She gave it to us
after the accident so that we could leave a car at Uzès and
need only ever take the train to get there. So I still drive
my children of today in a car in which my children of
yesterday were frequently driven by their grandmother.
The hyphens that link the older two with the younger
two are becoming fewer; the Peugeot is one of them, as is
the cleaning woman who comes to us in Paris for a
couple of hours on Saturday afternoons, and with whom I
never evoke the least memory although she was already
with us in the time of Mathilde and Elise. Her presence
provides an element of coherence which we will miss
when she retires, and that is bound to be soon.

We were starving when we got back from the
Cévennes so we went to gorge ourselves with pizza in a
pizzeria at Uzès, which had once been a butcher's shop
where I had ordered minced beef for the successive

babies. I had stopped using it when a supermarket
opened nearer to our house a few years ago, six or seven,
and I have never been back since, except very occasionally
to buy a ready-made meal and to chat to the woman who
had been the butcher and now ran the restaurant.

I was so wrapped up in the happiness of that evening
that I was not thinking of anything else as I sat at the
table in the pedestrianized road, sating my hunger with
my children and their friends, watching them: so sweet
and so pink after their gambolling in the streaming water.
The owner came to chat to me and, as the children were
getting fidgety and beginning to behave badly, I sent
them off to wait for me a bit further away. 'When I see
those two there,' she said to me, 'they are so, so alike all
four of them.' Those four words 'all four of them' were
the culmination of the whole day.

I would so love to write to you more often. Sometimes
I do not have the strength to, sometimes I do not
measure up to the demands of – on the one hand – this
terrible hardship and – on the other – a life which is rich
despite itself. At the moment the country is marking the
fiftieth anniversary of the round-up at the Vel'd'Hiv'*, I
am struck by, disconcerted by the matter-of-fact tone of
the articles published. There is a horizon, perhaps one
that can never be explored, beyond the immediate
question of responsibility. Never explored? Do you

---

* The Velodrome d'Hiver was a cycling stadium into which Jews were
rounded up during the Second World War. They were kept there in
appalling conditions and stifling weather, with no facilities. From there
they were transported by train to concentration camps.

remember Annette Muller's book *La Petite Fille du
Vel'd'Hiv'*. She went to see it forty years later. The death
of my two daughters is not reduced to a problem of road
safety either. I'm going to tell you: my sister-in-law's car
was rammed on the motorway by the great powerful
Toyota of a young man who was driving very quickly.
When my sister-in-law managed to regain control of her
Renault 5 and to stop on the hard shoulder, she was
pleased to have come off so lightly and she and her
husband turned round to smile at the children to reassure
them. Their nieces were no longer on the back seat. It is
that moment, the moment in which the smiling, relieved
adults turn round to the children in their care and
discover that they have disappeared from the car; it is
that moment that we must examine because we do not
understand it at all, all the other details are fortuitous.

Yesterday, while the children were trying to keep their
balance on the slippery pebbles, battling against the
current with water up to their waists, already imagining
themselves being carried down to the little waterfall that
they called Niagara, their skin pimpled by the cold but
even so they wanted to stand in the wake of the source
which sprang, freezing, from under a bush so that they
could feel the contrast with the surface of the Gardon
which had been warmed by the sun – I would have liked
to go back to the bank to get my camera from my basket.
But none of the things that I was feeling then could be
photographed. I have the same feeling of shallowness
when I tell you about the death of the little ones (the
older ones) as I do when I photograph the life of the
little ones (who are bigger now than their elder sisters).

At the same time I would hate to die without having
tried to explain to you what happened before you knew
me. In the end, I took the pictures yesterday anyway. But
apart from me, who will hear the shrieks of joy when
they look at them? Who will feel the chill and warmth on
the shivering little tummies? And the wobbling pebbles
under their feet? And the fear of being carried over the
waterfall, which I had made a point of not telling the
children was not in the least bit dangerous? As we don't
know what we are living, we don't know what we are
losing. Anne Parillaud made an interesting remark in this
week's *Paris-Match*: 'I don't do what I want, I do what I
am,' she said and added later that she did not know who
she was.

I am trying to make you concede that Mathilde and
Elise were just as alive in Auteuil the day before yesterday
as their brother and sister were in the Gardon yesterday.
There is no difference between the four of them, except
simply that two are dead and the other two are alive.
That is a fact. It is an inexplicable fact but one that
translates itself into several others that break my heart,
like never being able to get a 'large families' railcard. I
have never had four children. And yet, at that pizzeria
yesterday, quite spontaneously, the owner saw four of
them.

27 July 1992

*W*hen we see each other the real life of today helps
me to bear these visits to what was not a real life of
yesterday. When I learned this morning on the telephone
that, contrary to my expectations, you were going off on
holiday again for a week, I immediately decided against
writing the letter that I am now actually writing. I
constantly need the presence of others. Some people
make a point of owing nothing to anyone. I make a point
of owing everything to everyone.

Have I already spoken to you about Raymond? He was
in my philosophy class at school, he was a bachelor for a
long time and was my most treasured friend until his
marriage, which I heard of thanks to a little note that I
received when I was on holiday in Noirmoutier: I can still
see myself reading those lines under the pine trees. The
announcement of that marriage rang in the end of my
youth. Thankfully, Raymond married very late! I wrote to
him recently about something or other, the lorry-drivers'
strike perhaps, and when I had signed the letter I
suddenly thought that I must have written to him after
the girls had died, even though I saw a lot of him at the
time, and I asked him in a postscript whether he could
lay his hand on that letter easily. I received it this

morning. There were five letters going from the 10th of
May (less than two weeks 'after') up till Christmas. The
first thing that struck me when I read them was that
these letters were the inviolable property of the person to
whom they were addressed. I felt just as intrusive reading
them as I would have done if someone else had written
them. The second powerful impression was the answer to
the question I had been asking myself by asking
Raymond to seek out these letters for me. It was obvious
that I had transformed myself into my own guardian
during the months that followed the accident. On the
10th of May, for example, ten days after their death, I
wrote: 'Raymond, will you be in Paris on 20 May? Could
we spend some time together? I won't have anyone with
me that day, and I don't want to be alone. I can't tell you
anything more at the moment: it is a colossal task just
thinking one day ahead. Yesterday Laurent and I went to
a restaurant for the first time, and I must have read the
menu for twenty minutes before I understood what was
on it.' And I ended the letter by commenting: 'I was
terrified before starting this letter, and I'm already feeling
better.'

So I chose my own baby-sitters and they were useful to
me. In another letter which is not dated but surely came
shortly after the former, I wrote: 'You must have been so
tired last night! I'm so desperate to talk. When I got
home after those hours of monologue I went to sleep
without sleeping pills for the first time and woke at about
five in the morning; I waited until it was time to get up
with a sort of peacefulness which I surely owe to your
patience.' I was conscious of the weight with which I was

burdening my friends, but I also knew that I was
lessening their pain by allowing them to have a beneficial
effect on my own. At the same period I also wrote this to
the same person: 'Raymond, I'm frightened of the street
at the moment, I'm frightened of anything that isn't in
the room that I'm in. But as soon as I'm feeling a bit
better, I will come to see you.'

In another letter I say: 'I have started writing again.
Strangely, writing is like receiving without giving
anything. I'll talk about this more sometime.' I probably
never said anything more about it to him, and I have no
idea what I meant. I hope that it is not true.

On the 30th of May (exactly a month after their
death), I announced to him: 'I'm going back to live in the
Avenue Mozart in two weeks' time. Until then I'm
gathering my strength and sorting through the children's
things.' Further on: 'I'm beginning to miss the children.
I'm also beginning to get glimpses of this terribly long
life that I must now live with lead weight in my heart.'
And I wrote about a book by Bergson* that he had given
me to read: it had slipped from my hand. Too far away,
all that was too far away.

So we went back to live in the Avenue Mozart. The
sorting was over. We had to go back and sleep in our
bed, in our room, next to the children's room which
would be silent for ever. We did it. Catherine and
Nathalie had put flowers on the balcony and filled up the
fridge. All we had to do was to water the petunias, the

* French philosopher

geraniums and the rose bushes. To eat the mangoes. We
wanted to repaint the girls' room. Marguerite Périer,
Laurent's godfather's wife, and her daughter Francine had
buckled down to it as if to some appalling task that could
not be avoided. They gave each other encouragement as
they stood on their step-ladders. They washed, filled in
and sanded down the walls and ceiling. And painted it all
in matt Gauloise blue and white gloss. All except one
place. One evening when I came in I found them in the
sitting-room with a glass of whisky. 'Vève, there's
something on the wall that we can't paint over.' They had
indeed spared one strip of wall, a vertical strip over which
they had not been able to persuade themselves to pass the
paint brush: a chart, marked out in pencil, showed
Mathilde and Elise's heights, measured every six months
from the moment they could first stand. I found our diary
and made a note of every mark. Marguerite and Francine
could paint now.

Only a few months passed before Francine Périer died
in turn in her car, squashed by a lorry that was too tall
for the Trocadéro tunnel and had toppled over trying to
get into it anyway. At the funeral, Marguerite, who had
already lost another of her daughters, walked about
amongst her friends with me, arms linked together, and
she introduced me to everyone: 'You see this young
woman? She is like me!'

26 July 1992

By digging through my cardboard boxes I have found my letters to and from Laurent dating back to the summer of 1980, the summer without children. If I can reveal those that I sent to Raymond, I cannot hide those that Laurent and I exchanged.

The most striking thing about them is the simplicity of our exchanges. We were apart because I was making the most of the school holidays. I wrote to him: 'I will be there on Sunday morning. If you get some addresses for the dog, could you get things moving a bit by making some phone calls, and arranging for us to see some people? I've thought that if I get pregnant this month, I will be on maternity leave from February so the question of the pooch problem won't arise till then. I'll leave you the papers for the car which is still at the garage because I left the house too early to go and pick it up. I've taken my manuscripts to Grasset, for the little books. We'll see. Big, big hugs, my darling.'

A letter from Laurent: 'My darling wife. I'm going to bed all alone this evening, feeling a bit depressed, a bit melancholy. I think that when I go to bed I will close my eyes and then open them again immediately and find myself in your arms, having abolished the intervening

time. But I'll be too impatient to get to sleep. So I'm
writing to you in tears just so that I can feel as if I'm
with you straight away. The days are so hard without
you. I think about you the whole time. About how gentle
you are, how tender we are. There is no longer any other
hand except yours in the whole world that I can hold to
reassure me, to make me believe that I am still living for
something. [. . .] Is there still something, something
more that I can do for you? Is there anything else that
you need or will you never need anything?'

It is no good. I cannot bring myself to quote the most
impassioned passages. And yet, when I read them just
now I really wanted to show them to you. Laurent's love
is mine. It is my treasure. It will die with me, having
made me live.

I also like to see how I love him, in turn. A month
later, I was already pregnant and I had prolonged my
holidays with my mother. 'I don't want to talk to you
about the children. It does you harm without doing me
any good. What can I say and how can I stop myself
talking? Here we are, my love, the two of us, orphaned
by our children, and I still see you through my eyes of
twelve years ago, I can't believe that my beautiful young
husband has known such heartbreak. The other day when
you flew over the farmhouse at the controls of the old red
Cessna, I was on the path behind the river and I jumped
up and down, waving my arms and saying: "It's Laurent!
It's Laurent!" My eyes were full of tears because before I
used to say: "quick! Look! It's Daddy! It's Daddy!" and so
many arms would have been waving. In your last letter
you asked me about my love for you, you asked in your

own way, so painful and urgent, so absolute, which makes
me feel as if I will never be up to it and that my modest
passion – even if it is the purest thing I have – will only
seem like a gulp of water swallowed too quickly to
quench your thirst. [. . .] What your wife of 33 can offer
you is precious little compared to what is lost with
Mathilde and Elise. Oh, my love, how will I manage to
gambol along the corridor when you come home, to
admire your prowess, I felt so alone and so stupid, on my
little path, a poor old fan in tears: "It's Laurent! It's
Laurent!" [. . .] Sometimes I think, it's not going to
work, that I will snap under the pressure of the nut-
crackers. At other times I think that in four or five years
we will be in a warm, vigorous little world again and that
it won't matter if you or I cry into our pillows at night.
My individual destiny is now no longer running, you
know that. What I want is to be a little band of people
who love you, soon. And now, with my nose in my
soaking wet hanky, how am I supposed to talk to you
about the work in the bathroom? I've enclosed a list of
things the plumber should have done. Never mind if he
hasn't started. Without the children, what does it matter?
I hope that pup is well.'

   Exalted by mourning? No. The previous summer our
letters had the same tone. Here we are . . . I wrote to him
when I was in Noirmoutier with Mathilde and Elise: 'My
love, I feel like ringing you, not that anything's wrong
with me but I'm afraid that it's not great for you on your
first night alone at home. It really upsets me not having a
phone right here. I haven't got the strength to face the
night, with the wind blowing through the pinewoods, and

the strange solitude of this brightly lit cabin in this
nocturnal desert. Above all I don't want to be clingy.
[. . .] Mathilde can do a few strokes of breast-stroke.
Elise doesn't stop playing and bouncing around in the
water, she has it right up to her chin and lets out little
squeaks of joy punctuated with hiccups when she takes a
mouthful of water. I'm swimming a lot myself, carried
away by their enthusiasm and to keep them company.
[. . .] A big hug and lots and lots of kisses. I love you
terribly.'

Another letter which talks of Elise's nettle rash, of the
fact that I must take Mathilde in hand because she is
becoming a tell-tale, of the fishing on the spring tide . . .
and which ends with: 'I will call you this evening because
you are leaving tomorrow. I love you, and I hope you
have a good trip, and I hug you with all my heart and my
arms right round you, my love.'

There are no miracles. There is just this. The love that
nourished your happiness will nourish your pain.

18 August 1992

Yesterday I had supper with my brother-in-law
Christian at this very table. We get on very well and we
have hardly spent any time alone together since the girls
died, except for once, just a few days after the accident;
we went to a café and I told him that I was aware just
how much pain we were causing his family. He had no
blood link to our girls but he found himself, his
twenty-four year-old wife, his baby and his future
children at the heart of inescapable grief. His wife was
driving the car, his baby had escaped unscathed from the
accident which had killed his two nieces whom he, a
young doctor alone by the side of the motorway, had
pronounced dead.

You probably remember that it was he who told us on
the telephone. I have always thought of that telephone
call as the sign of insurpassable courage.

In his direct, intense and restrained way he told me
that at least once a month for the last twelve years he ran
back along that stretch of motorway. He told me again
about the moment when his wife had got the car under
control and he yelled 'Well done, Aline' before turning
round to the children only to find that there was only one
left, their own. That is when he walked or ran along the

motorway. He says that he established that they were
dead and beat the ground, screaming. He says that he
does not remember why but he slapped his wife when she
ran to join him, screaming. He remembers that the
emergency services were a long time coming, and that
someone – a man nearby – had helped him to cover our
daughters, one with a coat, the other with a blanket. A
woman was giving Aude her bottle. The emergency
services arrived from the other direction, so that the
motorway was blocked in both directions and the traffic
was brought to a standstill as far as the eye could see.
Our girls had to cross right over it. A woman was crying
and Christian was amazed by her tears but they helped
him a bit. 'I was the only person who really saw how they
were,' he told me. I did not ask him how they really were
by the side of that motorway. I might ask him one day.

I must get on with this account. In my last few letters
I was talking about my correspondence with Raymond
and Laurent. But it is agony to have to talk about the life
of drudgery that I led afterwards. It was such a painful
void. Whereas moments like this one . . . When Mathilde
was little she liked to look at the illustrations in *Snow
White* which terrified her. I say 'when she was little' as if
she were ever big. She turned the pages and pointed out
the hideous, hunch-backed wicked queen and kept
coming back to it. Now I am the one who turns the
pages and keeps coming back to the appalling images. My
Snow White is Mathilde.

And Elise? That is just it. One of them always masks
the other. A friend of mine who had twins told me that
she had never cradled one of her babies without feeling

troubled by the other one which was left in its cradle.

I would like to write about only those moments in which I do not feature. Me at home, them on the A1 motorway. Good. 'Let's get on', as I like saying in editorial meetings when people are losing interest and I am getting impatient.

So we came home on the 14th of June. My friends had put flowers in all the window boxes and filled the fridge with good food. I have probably already told you all that. Let's get on.

No, actually, what I also wanted to tell you when I talked about that supper with my brother-in-law last night was that as I listened to him I did not feel the terrible fear that those evocations always provoke in me: I listened to him, knowing that I would tell you everything. What he said to me was just passing through me. I was already telling it to you as I listened to him.

23 September 1992

*A*t about eight o'clock this morning one of the presenters on Europe 1 Radio rang Roman Polanski on the air. He asked him about the release of his film *Bitter Moon*. Was it easy to film his own wife 'from every angle'? The phrase was used twice, insinuatingly, and it bothered me both times. And, as usual, when someone veers right off course, they end up falling flat on their face. 'Your wife is pregnant, is the baby due soon?' 'January 1993', Polanski replies. 'You are fifty-nine, is this your first child?' I hold my breath. There was absolutely no pause between the presenter's question and Polanski's reply, but I could write pages about that fraction of a second because it was so distended. The question was disagreeable enough in itself, because no-one should be humiliated for their age, race, social background, all the factors which cannot be changed. Anyway, what can be done about it? There the baby is, heading for a life with a much older father, from whom people are already trying to separate it, condemning him as incompetent; they want to deprive him of his virility, of his candid joy, of his love, to make him bite the dust just in case, in case it does not actually matter to him already that he is getting older, that he is thirty or forty years older than his wife with his own decrepitude so close on the horizon. But in other respects the question was catastrophic, and it went far beyond its small-minded objective. 'I don't know what to say to you,' said the film-maker softly. 'My wife Sharon Tate was eight and a half months pregnant when she was assassinated . . .' When you want to hurt someone a little you can hurt them terribly. You aim for a small target under the belt and you strike the heart. And, over and above the person targeted, the memory of the dead.

Having said that, I enjoyed this dialogue. Because it made it possible to separate the elder child from the new one, and to evoke a pretty young woman and a baby who, even before being born, would know the world only for its monstrous marginality. And because it is so familiar to me. 'How many children do you have?' I have four children. But where? Well, on my family record book. It is not something that you show to everyone, I know, but they are there nonetheless. They are in the next edition of *Who's Who* too. The proofs of my biographical entry were sent to me, and I checked the spelling of those four beloved names, and dreamed about them for many minutes in my office. The rest was just a bunch of grey text. For a long time Laurent saw them featured on his social security card, of which I was so jealous. And when he received his new one last year, he said to me, amazed: 'Look! They've forgotten Mathilde!' We thought about it. No, 'they' had not forgotten her. But she had come of age, our daughter, in 1991: eighteen years old. A student probably. Fending for herself, anyway. Too grown up to appear on her daddy's entitlement card. Autonomous.

I am not sure that Polanski did not feel some joy in

evoking the presence of his eldest child, even if he had not planned to do so, when he was announcing the arrival of the next baby. At the end of the day, people are not always as hurtful as they mean to be.

13 October 1992

 This month the girls would have been seventeen and
twenty years old. I still love them, and it is them as
young girls that I love. There are other birthdays and
anniversaries to celebrate in October. Our son has been
invited round to a little neighbour's house for his ninth
birthday. My goddaughter will be twelve, my niece
thirteen, my nephew eleven, my mother celebrates her
golden wedding anniversary, although my father died
shortly after their silver wedding, then there is the five
hundredth anniversary of Christopher Columbus,
America, the seventeenth birthday of Mathilde's
godfather's son, on the very day of her twentieth birthday,
that is the month of October. In my heart, every time I
cross the street, buy a loaf of bread, turn on the
television, open the shutters or lay the table by myself, I
am making my children grow up, or rather I am allowing
my daughter of seventeen and my daughter of twenty to
grow up. On the 8th of October, on Elise's birthday, my
mother rang me at work; she wanted to speak to me on
the day. I know that she will also ring on the twentieth.
We love each other in our grief, our impotence, she who
made me and I who made my daughters. Aline has been
to the grave in Compiègne, my mother will go, my

mother-in-law too, we will go last, so that throughout the
month of October there are flowers laid there,
straightened, watered, touched. Every year Mathilde's
godfather sends an enormous white chrysanthemum; we
free it from its cellophane paper when we arrive at the
cemetery where it waits, wrapped up; it is our last gesture
in October.

Yesterday, I ran into the mother of a classmate of
Mathilde's. I was walking up the road with a neighbour
and I started to tell him who this woman was. I wanted
to evoke particular memories, which I would probably
have kept to myself if it had not been the month of
Mathilde's twentieth birthday. I wanted to talk about my
eldest daughter, without labouring the fact that her
birthday was just a few days later. But I must have gone
about it in the wrong way, told it too slowly, or perhaps
my story was just not interesting: my neighbour
interrupted me, he went on to another subject, I bit back
my anecdotes. It was sad, but his lack of intuition offered
me the one thing that I really accept: loneliness and
suppressed tears.

I should not forgo telling you about the year that
followed the girls' death. How shall I go about it? The
simplest thing would probably be to enumerate what I
did. We adopted a dog. Laurent took me to America.
That summer I learned that I was pregnant. I went back
to work. Over Christmas we took refuge in Italy. There
was the court case. I wrote a novel. I let everyone console
me. There were no supporting roles. Each one was useful.
Everything was primordial. Some things required
enormous effort. But we got the hang of it. We knew

that you could not suffer that much for any length of
time, that the paroxysm lasts only a few hours and that,
once those hours have passed, anaesthesia sets in.

I will go back to my list and will tell you just one
memory associated with each element.

The dog. We wanted a grey pointer: you know how
important beauty is to us, how much it helps us, builds us
up, reconciles us to the world. Having methodically
studied the breeds whose characteristics and looks would
suit us, we therefore decided to look for a Weimaraner.
In the end we heard of a litter which had been born in
the Limousin region. In the scorching heat of the first
few days of July we made the journey, alone in the front
of the 304 whose back seat no longer served any purpose.
We arrived hungry and thirsty at the château, where the
lady of the house met us on the steps. We played with
the puppies on the lawn, teasing them to put their gentle
natures to the test: since we were planning to have other
children, we needed to choose a particularly good-natured
dog. Under the crushing heat of the sun, we signed our
cheque and left with the baby Rochelle, whom you know,
without our hostess asking us in to drink so much as a
glass of water. Tired and dirty, we drove home. We felt
rejected, dejected. When you are unhappy you are never
far from being reduced to the state of a down-and-out.
You only have to be deprived of one glass of water and
there you are.

America. Laurent was attending the opening of a hotel
in Houston and, to divert us a little, his boss offered me
a ticket too. I had never accompanied Laurent on a trip
before: it was too much work and I wasn't keen to leave

the girls. Except, of course, on the 30th of April. There
was nothing to keep me at home now. In the wide open
spaces of Texas I did not suffer. The television was
relaying the Roland-Garros tennis tournament, which I
watched from my room. The hotel was magnificent, I was
proud of my husband. Then we set off for Mexico to visit
other hotels, with a view eventually to setting up a branch
of the chain that Laurent worked for there. It was
different there. The altitude meant that I could not
breathe easily, and this slight suffocation reawakened
another. When I went to explore mountain villages while
Laurent was working, I looked for my daughters
everywhere. The Indian children wore frilly dresses and
jeans with holes. I overtook them just to check whether I
recognized Mathilde or Elise in their dark faces. I saw
Laurent do the same thing in the streets of Mexico City.
One evening, he stopped on the pavement next to a
sleeping child, a beggar, and slipped some pieces of
chewing-gum into his open hand.

Pregnant. I knew that this would make everyone
happy. In the Trois Suisses catalogue I looked at the
pages that covered clothes for four and seven year-olds.
Then, as my strength came back to me, I leafed
backwards until I came to the pages for newborns.

The court case. Nothing.

A novel: I do not suffer when I write.

Christmas, Italy. We obviously could not stay in
Paris for Christmas. We did not want to see the
shop-windows nor did we want to spend the evening
with anyone, knowing that we would ruin the festivities
for them. We chose Tuscany and Rome. I must take

great care when I tell you about this journey. I hope I
will manage it next time. At the moment, I do not have
the strength.

21 October 1992

It is nearly All Saints' Day. We have not yet been to
Compiègne; we will probably go tomorrow, unless the
weather is too forbidding. And you? Do you go to your
father's grave at All Saints'?

Last night I was thinking that I would write to you
today, and I hoped that the day would never dawn.
Alongside the anguish of submerging myself in our
Italian trip – as I said I would in my last letter – was the
worry that I will end up overwhelming you. It seemed to
me that I was becoming increasingly terrifying, inhuman,
with the great black stream of my letters. A friend who
always used to have something cheering to say to me has
spoken to me in a different tone for the last couple of
months, peppering his sentences with *'ciao'*, *'bye-bye'* and
'salut'. Where do they come from, these words that
everybody uses? Last night, I thought there was nothing
beautiful about my life. When I woke the radio was
blaring out an interview with Dr Garetta*. The world
was a terrible place.

---

* Dr Garetta ran an organization which (knowlingly and for profit)
allowed the transfusion of AIDS-infected blood to patients. Hundreds
were contaminated during the years of his cynical management. There
was a huge scandal when this was uncovered.

So, a few days before Christmas in 1980, we took the
train to Tuscany. In ten days we hoped to visit Tuscany
and Rome, and to complete an Etruscan circuit. The
Renaissance, antiquity, the kilometres, exile and nothing
but the two of us to fuse all of this with the absence of
Mathilde and Elise. So that we should not set off entirely
alone, some friends lent us the guide books that they had
read on their own trip to Tuscany. I was five months
pregnant.

In Florence we rented a Renault 5! Those winter days
were short, so much so that we found ourselves back in
our hotel room at five o'clock, not knowing what to do.
During the day we went from masterpiece to masterpiece,
walking a great deal; many sites were closed for
maintenance work, but Florence is inexhaustible and so
were we. The Christmas shop-windows were very
different from the Parisian ones, not so focused on
childhood and toys, rather on *panettoni* and food. They
did not hurt us. Sometimes, for example in a tiny perfect
cloister that seemed small enough to fit in our little
apartment, I asked myself what I was doing there, storing
up these images that I would never give back to my
children. The times when I felt that I was just an empty
carcass were rare. More often, the beautiful images from
other centuries gave me the gift of a past so ancient that
the immediate past lost some of its power.

Sometimes Laurent had obsessions. Seeing the
mosaics at Ravenna, for example. The mountain roads
that led to them were snowbound and deserted. I was
cold in the Renault 5. I thought the car would break
down and that we would die of cold there. Then we

arrived at the first church. Dark. We slipped a 100 lire
piece into the light meter and lifted our eyes: from the
dome, heavenly creatures were looking down on us in a
stream of gold and glittering vegetation. And clonk, the
light went out. A hundred lire, paradise burgeoned green
again. We who went through life looking at the ends of
our shoes were at last lifting our heads to this Garden of
Eden. One hundred lire activated three minutes of a
golden eternity. Laurent was right. He knew what was
good for us.

At other times his obsessions were catastrophes! He
wanted to see San Marino, a strange republic in a little
enclave on the eastern coast, surrounded by fortified walls.
A wealthy, pagan place where we were to spend
Christmas night. But I wanted to go to Mass. I wanted
candles, prayers, Christians. I wanted to sing and cry, I
wanted vaulted ceilings, the cross, the crib! We set off.
The night of 24 December. Conjugal silence. A mask.
And then there we were near the sea in that closed city.
We ate in an ugly little restaurant. Slept in a bed-and-
breakfast in a sort of simply built garage which had been
transformed into a makeshift bedroom. The few passers-
by in the street said '*Auguri?*'* as they went by us, and I
said between gritted teeth: 'That's right, that's right,
auguri.'

Etruscan tombs. Couples looking at each other and
loving each other. Horses with fine hooves galloping,
happy and proud. Palid frescoes. Before going down into

* Season's greetings

the grotto, the guide jokes: 'Everything here is very fragile. Speaking is forbidden, so is breathing, giving birth and dying.' These bans created in us too great an echo.

Sometimes our excessive appetite for sites drove us to our limits. In a church in Siena, which we reached in mid-afternoon having had no lunch, we were overcome with the hysterical laughter of exhaustion. I can see us both leaning against a column laughing, laughing. The church was probably about to close. When we left we put away a historic pizza, 'Calzone di Giotto' – which has always remained for us 'Giotto's boxer shorts'*, rather than Giotto's slipper – stuffed with tomatoes, anchovies, ham, cheese . . . Giotto's colossal boxer shorts, obscene, filling and absurd. The childless parents stuffed their faces.

San Gimignano. The most beautiful room in the hotel, with windows opening onto the most beautiful piazza in the world. The two of us in the double bed, under the high ceiling.

And the journey to Assisi. I am buried in the *Michelin Guide* looking for somewhere to spend the night. Occasionally, I look out of the window at the hills, I lower the window to hear the sheep bleating in the distance. Then I dive back into the guide book and make suggestions to Laurent. Then I look up again. At the bend in the road, under the white sky of this beautiful winter's day, just over there, is Assisi. I am stunned. It is

---

* The French word for boxer shorts is *caleçon*, i.e. very like *calzone* which, in Italian, is slipper.

so beautiful! For a moment, I rediscover a familiar joy, the joy that the Earth, Creation, Man's harmony with his planet bring, if you will forgive me for being so pompous. The little village does not really lend itself to it. But for the first time, for several seconds, I am as I was before. For the first time I knew that I had a future. The world did not come down to the death of two little girls.

Rome. The 31st of December. We eat in a quiet trattoria. We go back to the hotel to bed. I go to sleep and I am woken by crying or car horns. Both. Midnight has just struck, we are propelled into 1981, my husband is crying.

4 November 1992

*W*e came back to Paris. Yes, I remember that in my
last letter I left you on the eve of the Pontifical Mass on
the 1st of January, but never mind the Pope. We came
back to Paris. The city seemed clean and orderly. I think
I started working again. I honestly have very few
memories of the first few months of 1981.

The case came before the court. The young man who
killed my daughters was recognized as the only person
responsible for the accident, and given a 1,200 franc
fine, and made to pay a further 500 francs for the
contravention. He left the court at the wheel of his car.
He was twenty-two years old; he is thirty-four now. We
never heard a word from him or his family. I think of
him as little as possible. Really very little. I would like to
tell you his name, but as he was granted amnesty a few
months later, I am not sure that I am allowed to. He was
called Jacques. Laurent and I each received 50,000 francs
for each of our daughters. If I remember rightly, the
grandparents received 10,000 francs each. The great-
grandmother, 3,000 francs. And Aline, who was driving
the car, also received some money, I do not remember
how much, but it was symbolically important because the
reasoning they used was unusual: the wrong for which it

compensated was the fact that it would be difficult for
Aline to keep her place in the family. It was the most
satisfying thing about the judgement. The funeral
expenses were reimbursed, which was a shame – I would
have liked that to have been left alone. But it is
apparently the custom. I also received a small sum to
compensate in some small measure for the abrupt closure
of my consulting rooms for speech therapy. As for the
school insurance, which the headmistress dealt with
unprompted, it gave us 5,000 francs for each of our
daughters, in compliance with the contract.

The family gave us the money they had received.
We bought a little studio apartment near the Place
de la Contrescarpe, and found an elderly tenant who
lives there still. From then on we had too much money
for our everyday lives. The salaries were for the two of us,
not the four of us any more. Buying a piece of furniture
or a beautiful ornament in the despair of a Saturday
afternoon made it possible for us to get through the
weekend. I do not know how I spent my time during the
week.

But listen to this: on the 23rd of April 1981, I took
my little suitcase and went to the clinic at La Muette
with Laurent. I climbed onto the bed in the labour ward.
I was in pain, and the physical pain linked to my internal
turmoil made me unbearable. I wanted to die. I moaned
the whole time and made a fuss. The doctor was taken
aback, called me 'my dear client' and lost grip of the
situation. Laurent stayed next to me, silent. He knew
everything. So I buckled down to my favourite sport, with
irrepressible vigour, fury even. The baby came quickly and

I turned to Laurent: 'Is it a girl or a boy?' A girl. A little girl. My girl.

Silence. She is blond, fair, slight, rounded. There she is in her pale green sleepsuit, curled up on her father's lap. I look at them both. Silence. The door opens a fraction; it is my mother. 'Mummy, it's a girl, Mummy, it's a little girl.' Elvire. That one, you do know.

11 November 1992

I would have liked to end this account there but there
are still things that you want to know. And yet I am
dragged into the great chasm of the past. Yesterday was
my birthday and, on impulse, I went out to lunch at
Virgin's with a colleague. He suddenly became arrogant,
aggressive, wrapped up in his own world and casting
aspersions on mine; and I was unable to stop him despite
my pleas for moderation. I still have not recovered from
it. Those situations in which my confidence is betrayed,
in which a friend no longer feels anything, barks at me
across the table, in which – after making desperate efforts
to stop him, but feeling that he was increasingly rigid,
increasingly mocking – I say to him: 'that's enough now,
you're hurting me, that's enough' in a tone I would expect
to use to an enemy; those situations rekindle the betrayal
of twelve years ago and trigger similar emotions. I put
Mathilde and Elise's raincoats on. In their overnight bags
they have their clothes and the little books that they like.
They are going to see their grandparents, it is a happy
Wednesday afternoon. They will be ejected from the car
and they will die. Twelve years later, on my birthday, I sit
down to eat with someone familiar. And because it is
him, I do not spot the danger. When I do see it, it is

already upon me. Back then, the young man in the
Toyota stopped after the accident and took a jointly-
agreed insurance statement form from the glove
compartment. He had not seen that my daughters were
dead as a result of his driving. Innocence.

What about lunch at Virgin's? There is no point in my
telling you about it. I would only exaggerate the disparity.
I do not really understand any more myself. Nor how it
could have happened, nor how I know that it is
irreparable. It just happened. This friend was free for
lunch and so was I. You sit down opposite someone and
you know that every time you look up from your plate
you will come across their gaze, benevolent, attentive,
kindly: in short, making the world a better place to be.
Stendhal wrote that the heart can make anything seem
important, can put the fall of an empire and the dropping
of a glove on the same set of scales. But I have always
wanted to be reasonable. Francine Cicurel (another
Francine, whom I have possibly not yet mentioned)
claims to like this ability I have to expose myself utterly
to what people call human relationships. Until now, they
were simple: I looked after my enemies, my friends
looked after me. My confidence has never been betrayed.
I slipped my hand into other hands and I have never had
to withdraw it. But there I felt the hand guiding me
towards the opaque darkness of abandonment. I did not
know how to withdraw my own. In fact, after lunch, far
from turning my back on him, I came up with a feeble
little phrase like: 'don't worry, it doesn't matter.'

That evening, sitting round the cake, my sister, my
mother, Laurent, Elvire and Gauthier formed a rampart.

When I got back from the office, Elvire was on the
telephone, turning down an opportunity to babysit for a
neighbour's children with obvious regret: 'I can't, it's a
shame, but it's Mummy's birthday . . .' her first baby-
sitting job! She would so liked to have done it . . . But I
could not be left alone that evening. She already knows
that when you have the choice between hurting someone
and not hurting them, you have to choose not to hurt
them.

In fact, she knows something that very few will ever
know: she knows that we have that choice.

You tell me that you do not really understand the
precise circumstances of the accident. I am loath to go
back to it, but I want to tell you everything that you want
to know. Aline was driving the Renault 5 on the
Autoroute du Nord, her husband next to her. The
children were sleeping on the rear seat, Mathilde on the
left, Elise in the centre, and the baby Aude in her car
seat on the right. Aline was nudged on the left-hand side
by the Toyota which was overtaking her. Flank to flank.
She was thrown to the right and bumped into the crash
barrier. The door did not open. Mathilde and Elise, who
had been sent to sleep by the cordial I had given them to
stop them being car-sick, went out of the broken
window. 'I saw some coats falling,' said the driver of the
car behind. Those coats were Mathilde and Elise.
Mathilde had head injuries. If I have understood it
correctly, Elise was thrown into the crash barrier, across
her tummy.

Earlier, I was on my own with Elvire: Laurent is in
St Petersburg and Gauthier is spending the night at a

friend's house. I took my daughter to McDonald's at her
request. A blond woman, who was there with her
husband and two children, stood up: 'Don't you recognize
me? It's Madeleine.' She had been the children's first
babysitter. It was the first time we had seen each other
again. I introduced her to Elvire, and she knew from the
newspapers that I had a son too. Her lips and chin
trembled, her eyes filled with tears. We chatted for a long
time, and our hamburgers went cold. When we left I
went to a fairground shooting range with Elvire, we fired
at balloons and won a pin badge. Then I drove her home
and parked the car. On the pavement, in the darkness,
the reflection of the street lights made her eyes shine. She
was crying. She had not known her sisters, and along
comes someone she has never met before and will never
meet again, but who talks about 'Mathilde's straight,
square haircut with the fringe'. A stranger who knows her
own sisters, her elder sisters, whom she will only ever
meet thanks to these brief resurrections, by chance, across
a table in McDonald's. 'And Elise,' she says, 'she's been
forgotten.' We held each other close. Yes, my Elise has
been forgotten. I think about her. I call her my 'Lilou' as
I used to. I put her vest on and run after her to put on
her pyjamas which she does not want on. She laughs, I
catch her, she is a sturdy little thing, I win, and there she
is dressed. No one remembers her. She has lost. She died
knowing how to spell a few syllables, still wetting her bed
at night. She died with her milk teeth. Elvire goes to
sleep next to me, we sleep together, in each other's arms.

1 December 1992

When a friend causes you distress, it is like civil war.
You have to fight your compatriot and you have not been
taught how to. I wake in the middle of the night steeped
in my unhappiness. I dreamt that a snake was rising out
of my throat. After the death of the children, we
devoured our reserves of vitality in order to survive, and I
knew that they would never be reconstituted. I have
watched my next children grow haunted by the thought
that something might happen to them; I knew, and had
plenty of proof, that I could no longer face up to
anything. But I had not foreseen that I could be touched
in any other way than through my children, nor that
every kind of reserve would have been exhausted. Not just
those that sustained my maternal love. It would be better
not to love anyone, but I have never in my life done
anything without loving someone.

4 December 1992

T· he terrifying absence of my daughters, which has
been amplified by these letters, engenders a real feeling of
panic: to lose someone else. Do you know, it is that that
this famous argument awakened. To lose someone else.
In fact, since then the bursts of anxiety that have swept
through me remind me very much of the years of grief.
They come and take possession of me, I know that they
will pass and, when they pass, I know they will come
back so I do not benefit from the respite. I was on my
own with the children yesterday evening, as I am when
Laurent is travelling, and I rang Francine Cicurel and
asked her to join me for an hour before going to bed. I
like having friends to supper with me on those evenings
when I do not feel sure of anything. Her ring on the
doorbell at the agreed hour. Her footsteps on the stairs.
Her smile. 'It's the emergency doctor,' she says laughing,
and we hug each other.

When I met Francine, our daughters had been dead
four months. Her daughter, Liora, just eight days after
mine. She had published a little letter in their local rag,
evoking this twelve-year-old girl, with her US bag on her
back, looking at hair slides in the shop-windows of the
local *parfumeries*. She lived two streets from us. Mathilde,

Elise and Liora very probably passed each other on the
pavements, in the shops, on the pedestrian crossings. All
three of them are dead. I responded to Francine's letter
and we met. It was like love at first sight. When she is
not here, because she is a linguist who is much in
demand and travels a lot, the area feels deserted. I love
her family, her husband, her children, her books, her
writing, everything that she touches. When I am with
Francine I never suffer, because she is the centre,
everything else is peripheral. When I gave the name
Alma to the paper that I created and edited eight
years ago, it was partly because at the time Francine
harboured a fascination for Alma Mahler. I wanted to
share this secret with her, to dedicate my paper and
my work to her. When we met, her youngest daughter,
Ilana, was the same age as Mathilde. She is here, this
young girl of twenty, as Mathilde is in another place.
She loves Elvire, who loves her. They play the flute
together. When Elvire was born, Francine came to the
clinic to see me and to see her. She was the first of my
children that Francine would know. Until then we had
only been able to speak of children that could never be
known. There, in my hospital room, Francine took my
third daughter in her arms and spoke to her in her
voice that was both soft and full of enthusiasm. I can
hear her: 'But do you know that you're the prettiest
baby in the nursery?' And yesterday evening, when
she discovered Elvire and Gauthier creating a rumpus
in my bed as they always do when their father is
away, she said in the same voice: 'Oh, I see. You're just a
couple of babies really.' They squirmed and smiled like

two babies in their cradles in reply to these words of love.

When I met Francine she only had two of her three children left. Jeremy was ten, Ilana eight. Liora was twelve when she died on the pedestrian crossing in front of her house. I went in, and the two children looked up at me, thanking me for the chocolates, looking me straight in the eye with open faces; they had none of the complication of children who do not want to say hello or thank you, who do not want you to do anything for them while all the time making sure that you are doing things for them; they were straightforward and welcoming, exactly like my daughters. What remained of my daughters was living there, perfectly incarnated in Jeremy and Ilana. The first time that I went to see Francine, I had taken photographs of the girls in my handbag just in case. We showed each other our photographs awkwardly, like cripples showing each other their mutilations, to use the formula that Francine used later. She in turn came round to see me, but did not find any children there to step forward and welcome her.

Evoking Francine makes it easier for me to go back to the fifty-first week of grieving which saw the birth of Elvire. On the 29th of April I went home with her. I settled her in the cradle that her godmother had lent me. And the next day was the first anniversary of the death of her sisters. The doorbell rang: Nathalie brought me three little bouquets of flowers, three identical bouquets except that Mathilde and Elise's were colourful and Elvire's was all white. She stayed by my side. I suckled my daughter while I spoke to Nathalie about her big sisters. There were beads of sweat on Elvire's blond head: was she too hot suckling? It was actually my tears that were flowing over her head.

How can I explain so many strange things? In that same apartment, the four of us lived. Then the two of us. Now, the three of us. Elvire's health made it possible. She was like Ariadne's thread, the vital link. She made it possible for her sisters to die and to exist at the same time. Later, she would protect her younger brother too.

9 December 1992

You came round to supper yesterday with some
friends. On the sideboard in the dining room we had set
up the crib that Elvire had asked for as a Christmas
present this year. I could not explain the whole story
to you yesterday evening. On Sunday I went to the
Saint-Sulpice area with her and we chose the figures
one by one. I was surprised that she should want a
crib at eleven and a half. My mother has kept our one,
which our four children have set up every year at her
house. I have always thought that when my mother is
no longer here, the crib would come to me for my
grandchildren.

So there I was, anyway, in the shop with Elvire. We
chose a peasant woman with some real wool, the wood-
cutter with a real piece of wood, the shepherd with his
cape billowing in the wind, holding onto his hat with his
left hand, the sheep, the magi, the camels, the holy
family, the stable itself. Then Elvire said: 'I also want two
angels to represent my sisters.' Yesterday evening, then,
you went past this crib, you even found it a bit moving,
that sort of thing is so traditional! But I wanted to catch
your sleeve and show you what you could not see: the
two kneeling angels, put there by a younger sister who

knows nothing of the elder two, but who struggles to involve them in our daily lives.

Recapitulating the past feels more and more difficult, more and more artificial and dangerous for me. I have probably already told you: I have never felt any continuity between my life with 'the little girls' (known later as 'the big girls' even after Elvire and Gauthier were older than they had been) and my life with 'the little ones'. Does anyone ever really confront the contradiction between life and death? Often I felt their life was so powerful that I would tell myself that they could not be dead; but just as often their absence seemed so complete that I no longer believed I had known them. So much so that Elvire's battle to bring them to life, to bring them into our home, is a solitary battle in which I ought to be her greatest ally; instead I look on, petrified. I adore her for carrying on this battle, I adore her in the religious sense of the word. But I do not feel as if I am helping her.

At the moment there is a lot of twaddle spoken about what babies can perceive while they are in the womb. These articles espouse the theory of the extra-lucid foetus. For nine months my baby heard nothing but tears and cries for help. When I brought her home, and for the first three years of her life, she had to put up with a mother who was certainly tender, but so distant . . . so absorbed in other lives. When I was pregnant I wrote to Bettelheim telling him I was worried: was it right to give life to a child in those circumstances? He answered: 'I am happy that you have done the only sensible thing you could: had a child. And I hope that you will have others as soon as possible. You will raise them in an atmosphere

of great anxiety, which is absolutely normal and cannot be
avoided.' This last sentence had an instantaneous and
definitive liberating effect on me. I was entitled to my
stupor. Mathilde and Elise had left with their raincoats,
their satchels, their lunch-boxes, their songs, everything.
And there was Elvire, fifty-one centimetres long, with her
sleepsuits, her feeds and her Moses basket. She needed to
get back up to her birthweight of 3.3kg. She did. But it
took some time.

All the same, the first time that I went out into the
street pushing her pram I was the queen. The queen! I
walked all the way up the street to where my mother
lived as if I was being cheered up the Champs-Elysées. I
had my hands on the handle of the pram and I was
pushing it, do you understand? I was no longer empty-
handed, swinging my arms, as I had for that whole year.
When I reached the square with the baby it was more
difficult. I got bored sitting on a bench. I was used to
waiting at the bottom of slides, cleaning eyes filled with
sand, doing up shoelaces. But my mother often joined
me, and brought me out of my torpor. And everyone who
had wept for Mathilde and Elise with us thronged round
Elvire, their exultation working on me gently. Our
paediatrician told his wife, who was Elvire's godmother:
'They've had the same baby three times.' The similarity
between them mattered a great deal. I needed this
minimum of familiarity. Yet, even there, social pressures
were brought to bear: if I had not been 'raised' by
Bettelheim, I would probably have forbidden myself to
look for the resemblances, for that source of comfort.

Yesterday you told me that the programme you are

producing may be saved. This morning you told me on
the telephone that it would not. Every episode I have to
face gives me the same painful buffeting. I know just how
much effort it takes to forge ahead. During the first few
years I was anaesthetized: a bomb had fallen on my
house, I was no longer afraid of anything. Now, it is
quite the contrary. Your programme is finishing and the
fact that something else now has to be created, to be sold
to the stations, the idea of the exquisite skill that will
have to be spent on it, exhausts me. Even if I am not the
one who has to provide it.

23 December 1992

I think that part of my reticence in writing to you
from now on, the fear that is always with me, derives
from the fact that at this point in my letters, Elvire is
there, alive. The beloved, grown-up Elvire who set about
reading one of my books yesterday. It cannot have
fascinated her because she abandoned it after three pages
. . . writing 'about her' seems indiscreet. When Mathilde
and Elise were alive, I would not have written anything
'about them'. I would not have authorized myself to,
believing that they alone should be in control of their
lives. You only have to see how little I tell you about
Laurent.

For the first three months of her life, Elvire had a
mother who was completely 'stoned', as we would have
called in when we came back from Chicago. But a
mother who was also devoted to her. I can remember in
Uzès when she was three months old, I could make her
laugh just by raising my eyebrow. I held her in the crook
of my arm, I responded to her expressions and we made
each other laugh. I breast-fed her for six months. When I
gave her her first bottle of vegetable broth, she drank it
readily, she trusted me, but she brought it back in two
hiccups a minute later. I put her back to the breast.

Sadly, two teeth had broken through: while our eyes were
speaking to each other during the feed, in her excitement,
she inadvertently bit me. So I had to wean her anyway.

In the autumn I went back to the Centre as a speech
therapist. We had enrolled Elvire at the crêche, unlike
her elder sisters: it seemed to us that her survival would
be better guaranteed in a professional environment. As
soon as she arrived, and despite the efforts we made to
adapt her to it gently, this healthy, pink and amiable baby
revealed herself to be asthmatic and stopped growing.

I took her away with me to spend the break for All
Saints' Day at Françoise's house in Creuse. I was stopped
at the toll booths on the motorway: my road tax had
expired. We had bought the car in August and had been
misinformed: I thought I was exempt from road tax
because more than half the year had elapsed. I was made
to pay more than three times the value of the road tax, or
– put another way – a fine that was twice what had been
paid by the young man who killed Mathilde and Elise. I
wrote to the tax collector to tell him about this; he did
not reply and soberly banked the cheque that I had sent
with my letter.

Christmas was upon us. I had started campaigning for
improved road safety. In January, Francine and I stood
for our local by-elections with this as our one policy. On
Christmas night, Laurent got out his design drawing
materials again, the ones he had used when he was
studying in Chicago. I must have told you how much I
loved him, bent silently over his desk, with his crayons,
his tracings, the sliding rulers and the tall stool. He
designed a poster for me for my electoral campaign. We

had it printed. And on the evening of the first of January, we put Elvire to sleep in her carrycot on the rear seat of the car, next to the posters and the brushes, we stowed the buckets and the paste in the boot of the 304, and we set off, with a map of Paris in our hands, to cover all the notice boards given over to the election.

That was twelve years ago. Tomorrow I will be spending Christmas at home, *en famille*. And the New Year in Creuse with Françoise

Uzès, 21 December 1992

When Elvire was born, my mother wanted to give
me a beautiful present. In an antique bookshop she came
across an anthology by Victor Hugo, bound in red leather
and called *Les Enfants*. I am writing to you from Uzès,
the book is in Paris, I am telling you this from memory.
It is a big, thick, gilt-edged book. My mother took it off
the shelf in the bookshop and opened it at the page
where the bookmark was: a poem told the following
story. A woman has a little boy. He is her pride and joy,
a beautiful, happy child – she adores him. But he goes
down with croup. It is serious, the child weakens, he is
dying, he dies. His mother wastes away. The husband is
at a loss as to what to do. The doctor advises him to give
his wife another child. She becomes pregnant and a boy-
child is born. But things are still not right, the mother is
pale, distant, looking after the baby in an absent way.
Then one day she thinks she hears a voice coming from
the pretty cradle. She moves closer, unsure, leans over it
in silence. And then, in that beloved voice, that she
cannot fail to recognize, she hears these words: 'It's me.
Don't tell anyone.'

My mother told me how the book had opened on that
page of its own accord. I have left the bookmark on that

page and have read all the other poems. They are about
children's lives, parents' lives. Children's deaths, parents'
grief. I liked reading all that. I liked the fact that Victor
Hugo was telling me all about it.

Now, I find it difficult to read. It all seems to run too
deep for me. During the day I try not to remember, even
just for a moment, that we lose those we love.

All the same, when Elvire was a baby, I was afraid of
nothing. I was in a sort of hallucination when I was with
her. At Françoise's house in Creuse she had an impressive
asthma attack. It was round All Saints' Day, there was
mist everywhere. I knew nothing about asthma, but
everything there was to know about accidental death. At
seven months, she would not have any accidents, and I
was still breast-feeding her a little, what on earth could
happen to her? She was breathing so badly, puffing like a
train. I held her to me day and night. Françoise called
the doctor. He examined my daughter on my knee: 'You
must go back to Paris straight away. Straight away. Her
heart could give up. Have her treated in Paris, I haven't
got the wherewithall here. Leave straight away.' I left.
The asthma calmed down during the journey. Eleven
years later, I still could not tell you where my lethargy
came from. A sense of abandon? Of impotence?
depression? An intimate conviction that I would never
keep any of my children? Or, the opposite, the
megalomania of a young mother perfectly tuned in to her
child? I was crazy. I did not understand anything much.
Yet, it was then that I wrote my second book, which is
hardly a sign of disorganization, and if you read it you
will not find a trace of that mindlessness. I remember

that we did the photo session for the picture on the cover
in our apartment while Elvire babbled in her playpen. I
do not look all that stupefied in the photograph. Life is
so complicated.

Neither do I understand why, the further I get from
the 30th of April 1980 in this account, the more I suffer.
During the period that I am describing at the moment,
all I needed was a moment of peace for the tears to roll
down my cheeks without a sigh. If I had to stand for
more than a few stops on the métro – I would cry. If I
had to sit in the kitchen while the soup warmed through
– I would cry. This morning I played a long game of
tennis with Laurent in the little club at Uzès, with the
mountains on the horizon and a beautiful cold sky
lighting up the scrubland. I played well, we were happy. I
put the rackets away in the boot and waited for Laurent
who was booking the courts for the next day. And there
are the tears, two warm streams, I am crying, crying,
where is Laurent? The most beloved beings die, or
change. You scour the horizon, they never come back.
Where should you go to find them? You are left alone in
the car, forgotten. The most beloved beings have
forgotten you. Then I saw Laurent's silhouette in his
tracksuit in the rear-view mirror. I wipe my face on the
sleeve of my sweatshirt. Laurent climbs in beside me,
imitates the accent of the man who does the bookings,
we are back on the road to the farmhouse, I laugh with
him.

I prefer telling you about my life now. I resent the
past, which was so hard to live, for pulling me backwards.
I resent you for not having been there then. I have to tell

you everything, you do not know anything. Telling you
about my life now is more interesting because you see it
at the same time as I tell it to you. You cannot change
anything about those years. When you rang me to give
me your love before I went away for the holidays, to tell
me that we would meet again in 1993, 'on the other side',
you were building a bridge to the future. Those who die,
those who change, send you over 'to the other side',
impoverished. Loneliness is the very devil.

1 January 1993

*N*ew Year's Eve last night in Creuse. Forty-five of us,
ranging in age almost exactly from seven to seventy-seven.
Nothing but kind, nothing but affectionate, nothing but
happy to dance. Telephone call from my mother bang on
midnight: I was thinking of her so much! Then I have
news of a friend I was expecting to see there: Françoise
tells me that he is not coming, his brother is dying of
leukemia. Going into the New Year with fewer loved
ones than in the old. Musset says: 'The soul is immortal,
yesterday is tomorrow.' I try to understand but it does not
make sense to me. You have to go into the New Year
with all your friends. Nothing is worth more than that.
You told me that you used to like reading my little book
about Christmas to Pierre right up until the year your
father died. A sentence that appears in it had then
become intolerable ('This year the baby Aude is here. But
this year Grandpa is no longer here'). I would no longer
write that now. A birth is not worth a death. Birth and
death are nothing to do with each other. No more than
East and West. And we spend our lives wondering what
the hell we are doing in the middle.

Ever since the moment when a friend was transformed
into a stranger, I feel as if I am being ejected into the

future. Rejected into the future, a stormy sea full of reefs.
Moored with multiple ropes, I stayed secure. One of the
moorings gave way, now the boat is heaving on the
others, everything is groaning, the boat is threatening to
sink. This mystery – the extraordinary impact of that
brief nightmare – reminds me of an adventure my little
Elise had when she was two. She was setting off by train
for Uzès with her grandmother (my mother-in-law). They
were as thick as thieves, those two. In the photographs of
her as a child, Granny even looked so like Elise that I
thought I had gone to an awful lot of trouble to end up
giving birth to my own mother-in-law . . . Anyway, I
accompany this little crew to the carriage door. There
were no TGVs then, can you believe how long ago it
must have been? My Elise is so grown-up now! There
she was in her loden coat. She was probably only just one
metre high. I explain to her that she is to sleep three
nights at Uzès with Granny, I take her thumb, her first
finger and second fingers: one, two, three times bye-byes.
There we are, the thumb, the first finger and the second
finger, and Mummy will come to Uzès. The thumb, the
first finger and the second finger, and Mummy will hug
her little one. OK, Elise? She stares at me fixedly,
without batting an eyelid. She is compact from head to
foot, focused, motionless as I squat in front of her; with
her eyes she puts herself at my mercy. In the palm of my
hand I can feel her hand with three fingers open and the
other two bent back against her pudgy palm. With my
free hand, I slip a lollipop into the pocket of her loden
coat. It is time. She climbs into the train with her
grandmother. A last look out of the window. Two days

later a letter from my mother-in-law telling me about the journey. Elise sits down in silence on her seat in the compartment (good, then; easy, even). She takes out her lollipop, her grandmother helps to unwrap it. During this manoeuvre, the lollipop falls to the floor. Germs! Red alert! The lollipop disappears into the dustbin. Then Elise begins to wail appallingly. Cajoling, hugs, promises, then scolding, threats, take a running jump: nothing works. Elise howls, splitting the ears of the other passengers, some of whom – on the brink of apoplexy – tersely give my mother-in-law tips on upbringing, and she sends them packing. Elise bawled like that, in the depths of despair, to the limits of her energy, her strength and her voice, all the way to Lyon. After which, 'as stiff as a soldier of the Empire', as Granny wrote so amusingly, she went to sleep on the moleskin seat.

You could conclude that: leaving Mummy is not that serious, but losing a lollipop is a catastrophe. Wrong conclusion. Leaving Mummy is a catastrophe. Which can be contained. But which explodes in all its magnitude if the lollipop falls and ends up in the dustbin. Thanks to these letters that I write to you, the same process has been set in motion for me. My daughters are dead. Both of them. The gentle older one and the little soldier of the Empire. Our own kindness and strength led Laurent and myself to the birth of Elvire and, later, Gauthier. Apparently, everything is fine. I go out quite confidently to have lunch with a guardian angel. The restaurant is nice. Twelve years have gone by like this, with these angels. I look at this one's face, I already know it well. I am no more on my guard than when I look at a familiar

landscape. But the contours alter. The most gentle
hollows become crevasses. The smile, a rictus. The voice
no longer hesitates. The sentences are punctuated with
sniggers. I leave the restaurant. The avenue is too wide,
the traffic too heavy, the office too far, home even
further.

Wherever I go, I will not find Mathilde or Elise. My
Elise who screamed for the love of me until she was
overcome by sleep! I must go into 1993. As Elvire has
often said since her birth: 'I will help you.'

3 March 1993

*H*ere I am after two months' silence! I came across
my four children looking out at me from a photograph
frame when I went to find an elastic band in the drawer
of the desk, and instead of taking the elastic band I took
out some writing paper.

I have just got back from our holidays and from the clinic:
I had an operation in Paris for the fracture to my thumb
that I received on the last day at La Plagne. My attempts to
stay upright on too fast a piste had ended like that. Nathalie
and her husband, and Laurent and myself brought our
children and their friends back on the trains which were
jam-packed. Then I left for the clinic at La Pitié.

I could not go on any longer after my last few letters at
Christmas. I wanted a real life now, cut off from the past.
For the first time, I adopted Laurent's technique, that of
the aviator Guillaumet*: to take one step at a time. I
wish I had never learned it.

* The courageous French aviator Henri Guillaumet crashed in the
Andes while delivering mail by air from Santiago to Buenos Aires in
1930. Only his incredible determination saved his life as he struggled
to walk back to civilization in sub-zero temperatures with no food and
in treacherous terrain.

Have I already told you about the spring day in 1980
when Michel, who was a journalist at *Le Monde*, took me
to visit Monet's house at Giverny? I had to go and pick
him up from the newspaper offices because he did not
drive. I was held up in the traffic at the wheel of the
304 in which, a few weeks earlier, the girls had sat
behind me. I talked to them and kept an eye on them,
smiling at them in the rear-view mirror. There was no-
one in the rear-view mirror any more. I was driving an
empty car. But in that traffic jam, I could feel my
daughters' arms around my neck, as they used to be when
they stood behind me to cuddle me and whisper in my
ear, and I told them that they had to leave me alone, that
I was going to pick up Michel so that he could take me
to a beautiful place, that Mummy had to do these things,
they were good for her, and that they should both –
Mathilde and Elise – let go, take their arms away, be
quiet and let me get on. It has been like that these last
few months.

Have I already told you that two weeks after the girls
died, when I went back to the office, I looked at my
friends, the colleagues I held so dear, as they sat in the
meeting room, I looked at them as if I was returning
from Vietnam, from a long and distant battle that none
of them had fought? They welcomed me, as I returned to
my homeland. It is important to reconstruct everything
now, when more than a decade has passed, to describe
how rupture and continuity, sadness and happiness, death
and life, mutilation and creation, exhaustion and
enthusiasm, loyalty and rejection, disgust and appetite
blend and nevertheless form a life. In 1980 I often looked

for someone who could tell me what sort of life I would
have in ten years' time. I am supposed to know myself
now. But these letters are a complicated task. I must both
live candidly and tell you what I am living, therefore not
candidly. Unless it is an even greater effort of candour.

31 May 1993

I am hesitating between two different temptations: to
write to tell you about something completely different,
and to write the lyrics of a song. I have been silent for
four or five months, I think. Writing songs is happy work
which reminds me of the time when I used to sign
editorials for *Elle*. I say that to avoid saying the time
when the girls were alive.

I have found some photographs of myself writing my
first book, with Mathilde on my knee. The portable
typewriter is in front of me and Mathilde is trying to type
too; she is one year old. I have very long hair. It is a
pretty sequence of photographs, but I looked at them for
a long time without feeling anything. It was all too long
ago. Real youth, the Olivetti typewriter, a tiny child . . . it
is in the past. Elvire and Gauthier are very interested in
these pictures. In them they see their parents and their
sisters as they have never seen them. I comment on them
without pleasure. It is really too long ago. I am only
interested in what remains to be done.

My resources are depleting: I do not even understand
anything of the past myself. And I do not understand
why people find it so fascinating. The other day someone
asked me: 'do your children know that you had other

children before them?' What did they think? That you
can hide that sort of thing? It was not the first time I had
been asked that question. It always irritates me. I tell
myself: 'If this is what stage we're at . . . If we even have
to explain that . . .' Elvire asked me when it was that we
had told her. We had never hidden anything from her
but one day she just understood. Just like that. There
were photographs of Mathilde and Elise in the house and
we talked about them freely. Elvire wore the clothes her
sisters had worn at the same age. It was obvious that she
was her parents' third daughter. One morning she joined
us in our bed and noticed that on the top of the book
case there was a radio with *Sesame Street* characters on it.
She wanted me to get it down for her: 'It belongs to
Elise.' 'Where is she?' 'She is dead.' That day those three
words said what they meant. I knew, without her
commenting on it, that she had given them their usual
meaning.

The memory of those years exhausts me. They were
certainly exhausting to live. Luckily, they seem to interest
you! I was crazy, groggy, KO. And yet: I wrote two
novels during those years. The years when we were alone
with Elvire. So? Do you understand it? My real life was
somewhere else. Having had two daughters, having lost
them, dragging through life with a third, smaller than the
first two, more intelligent than me, and the blondest of
the five of us, that was not my life. I found continuity in
my novels.

I was thirty-four, thirty-five, thirty-six years old. And I
was making myself start all over again. It was not the age
at which things should begin. I wanted to be well on in

life, and yet there I was. With a tiny child. A toddler, as the Americans say.

The worst thing about it was that I could not count any more. For that whole period, I could not do a single sum. I could just about count upwards from nought and remember my times tables. But as soon as I had to carry one, or there was a large number or the least complication, as soon as it went beyond complete automation, I had had it. I can just see myself in the shops, constantly baffled by the change I had been given. If I had given a 100-franc note to pay for 72.85 francs worth of vegetables, how much should they be giving me back, then? I would leave in a state of torment, sure that I had been robbed. It never added up.

I was pregnant again. It was Christmas 1982. Miscarriage. We bought the television. Life on the screen seemed more real to me than my own. An impression that has never left me. There we are, viewers in the calm of our own homes watching people struggling desperately on a stage. All of life on a stage.

And then pregnant again. For keeps, this time. My Elvire listened to the baby moving. The bigger I got, the more she clung to me and asked to be carried. At last a living sister? She would be called Madeleine. At the second-hand shop in Barjac in the Gard region, I found her a lovely antique tumbler with her initials on it: M.J. While I was waiting for her I read all of Apollinaire's poems to Madeleine.

My obstetrician listened to the heartbeat with his stethoscope. 'It's beating slowly. That's as it should be.' Scan. I was six months pregnant. I did not ask any questions. It was a fourth girl, I was going to be able to say 'my girls' just like before. I was content. A new maternity leave on the horizon. I was beginning to relax for the first time in this new life. It was at last, after four years of waiting, slipping gently into the former one.

Little by little, the words 'the heart is beating slowly, that's as it should be' came back to me. I had left them to sleep. Those beautiful slow-beating hearts, the hearts of athletes with quiet, well-spaced beats, which pulse ponderously; those hearts beat in the breasts of men. I knew it. You put your ear, your cheek onto a man's chest and that is what you hear. That is what defends you when you are a grown-up. I can see myself back in Dr Cohen's consulting rooms, pale and apparently in suspense, when it came to my eight-month check-up. 'You said that the heart was beating slowly. Is it a boy?' He asked me whether I really wanted to know. Yes! Yes, just so long as he confirmed that I was having a girl! 'I have written the sex of the child on the back of the scan papers that you have at home. Look if you want to.' I went home.

The apartment was light and empty. I opened the drawer, looked for my maternity folder and for the scan in its white envelope, I turned over the picture and read the sign. An arrow in the air on a circle. I had seen this sign ten times a day on the files of my speech therapy patients, I had written it so many times myself in the last fifteen years. But I did not know any longer if it meant a boy or a girl. Girl or boy. An arrow in the air. Girl or boy. Boy. Boy. I was expecting a boy. I was thirty-seven and I would never again say 'my girls' to mean the living children who were waiting for me at home.

1 June 1993

The children have asked us a hundred times whether they would have been born if their sisters had not died. I really hope so, but I just cannot say. The girls' death allowed me to be pregnant again, which I wanted anyway, to have other children, which I wanted anyway.

The fact that I was expecting a boy hoisted into the foreground a new kind of stupor, relegating the stupor of mourning to the background. You will have to believe it because I am telling you: a boy? I had expected everything except that.

I did not talk any more. I was watching women in the streets with their sons: how do you dress a boy? How do you have his hair cut? What sort of toys do you give him? And I imagined the unimaginable: a man rooted in the core of me. I was creating something other than myself. I was creating the other tribe. The fascinating, forbidden tribe. Having never had brothers or sons, all that I knew of men was mystery and temptation. And there was one of them there. I could not do anything about it, I had had no choice. I was carrying him. I was no longer expecting and carrying a child, but a man. You could have knocked me down with a feather.

Laurent was willing to call him Gauthier. As with the

girls, I wanted a name that had no equivalent for the
other sex. But whereas for the three of them we had
chosen names that had been borne by women who had
inspired the greatest artists (Stendhal, Beethoven,
Lamartine . . . and Apollinaire for the Madeleine I had
dreamed of), I wanted a name for my son which
embodied every quality I loved in men. Constancy,
clemency, courage, joy and modesty. One of the knights
of the Round Table was the incarnation of these virtues. I
was sure that, according to which version you read, he
was called either Gauthier or Gauvin. Since then I have
only been able to find him referred to as Gauvin. Never
mind. Gauthier it was.

Stubbornly I got my bag ready for hospital and, for the
baby, I put out only the white and pink layette that had
done for its sisters. I scoffed at the whole world and at
psychoanalysts in particular. This little man would be
born to a mother who would take him on eye to eye. He
would have to teach me everything. I only had a couple
of elementary ideas, basic theories which I stuck to
mutely. One of these theories was: I've got clothes for
three little girls in my wardrobes, we'll see if I really have
to go out and buy boy's clothes. My son would have an
identity before he had a label.

He was born. And he was so beautiful! Don't laugh.
He had such big hands, such big feet, like puppies' paws
which seem to supply them with endless resources for
growth.

For the six days that I was at the clinic, I did nothing
but look at him. Nothing else. Leaning on my elbow, I
watched him. As if he was coming from the horizon.

Like in those sequences from *Lawrence of Arabia* when a man on a camel is approaching, approaching, so slowly even though the camel is galloping, so slowly because he is coming from very far away and because the animal and the rider's clothes — hair and cloth — are barely distinguishable from the sand and the halo of burning air.

As I watched him I told myself that one day he would love another woman. I wrote about this to Bettelheim. He wrote back to say that the relationship between a mother and her first son was probably the least ambivalent of all. That you saw the girls who would one day be *loved* by a man and the man one day *loving* a woman. But that it rarely troubled people as early as the maternity clinic!

Nothing had changed. Gauthier, like all men, was mystery and temptation. My little boyfriend . . . did Laurent realize straight away? I was at last confronting him with an acceptable rival!

ʃ June 1993

I have never been made to feel powerless by my three
girls. At every moment of their lives I have felt
competent. With Gauthier, from the minute he was born,
I have needed other people. One day, just for a change, I
was watching him in hospital, and I suddenly saw his arm
take on that terrible colour, a sort of silvery blue, the
colour of death. I grabbed him and threw myself into the
corridor, thrusting him into the face of the first passing
nurse, convinced that his life was ebbing away, or rather
that cyanosis, suffocation, the end was triumphing
through his arteries. 'He must have been lying on his
arm,' said the young woman in her Turkish slippers, as
she rubbed his little hand to stimulate the circulation. If a
daughter of mine had had a blue arm I would have
moved her, babbling to her gently.

I was, I still am, staggered to have a son. Staggering
with amazement, and reeling with pride. For the last nine
years every time I say 'my son', I ask myself whether the
person I am talking to will believe me. Whether it will
take. What is more, everyone (except for Laurent who,
quietly and mischievously, watched a new stability
establish itself in the family) shared in my incredulity, all
those at least who had known me 'before'. 'How are the

girls?' people ask me almost every day. I tell them that
Elvire is fine, and so is Gauthier. Then they are
embarrassed, but it makes me smile. They are like me,
they think that this boy is the best joke of my life. I who
thought I could answer to the disappearance of two girls
with the birth of four, I was countered by the most
unexpected reality: a boy. A boy to whom Laurent had
given as a second name the first name of his uncle and
his great-grandfather, in an attempt to anchor him on the
side of the Vikings, which he had not done with the
girls. So I got in there myself with my father's name.
Gauthier knows all this without our having to tell him.
When he signs something, he writes 'G.J.L.' because G.J.
on its own would be his mother's initials rather than his
own. He adds his father's for good measure. Bursting
with pride. The original Yiddish mother. Oedipus? Well,
as long as the baby boy loves his mother . . . the story in
that vein that I feel closest to is the simple one of the
Jewish mother who rings the airport: 'Hello, Roissy
airport? When is it landing, my son's flight?'

   Elvire and Laurent came to collect us from the clinic.
While we were paying the bill and filling in forms, she
carried the baby and showed him off to everyone in the
waiting room. And then there we were in the car. She in
her seat, he in his carry-cot. We, the parents, in front.
No-one said anything. We drove dreamily through the
streets of Paris. Content. And, as we waited at a red
light, I heard Elvire's voice. 'There's two, Mummy, isn't
there.' She was two years and ten months old. I knew
what she had said but I insisted: 'There are two what, my
love?' 'There's two children.'

From the moment I got back to the house, my
problems with sums disappeared. There were four of us
again. I could do multiplications again, and divisions, and
work out how much the grocer owed me at the till. It
added up.

15 June 1997

*E*verything happened at once, in the space of three months. Gauthier's birth, the creation of a new movement on the subject of road accidents, the beginning of my political commitments and my change of career. I had ceased to be subjected to history, and I wanted to write it myself. Quite soon, I was expecting a fifth child which I lost dramatically in the early months; I understood the limits of my megalomania.

I must explain to you why I founded the *Ligue contre la Violence Routière**, but I am getting tired. Let me summarize. Acting militantly in this arena meant making painful gestures such as appearing on television and, effectively, saying: 'look at my face, look at the indignity of a woman who has lost both her children. This is what road accidents mean. Every year there are so many thousands of us with a face like this.' I would have liked to remain gentle and to have drawn the people who liked gentle women. Instead I confronted the road-hogs, the beeping horns, the screech of wheels, the scraping of metal, the ambulance sirens. A strange seduction strategy.

* Literally: the League Against Road Violence

Would I have liked to stay in the world of literature and poetry? I scrambled round administrative offices looking for statistics. Would I have liked to switch off and just be with my babies? I answered the letters of those who wrote to me about the deaths of their loved ones. Why? Because it was stronger than I was. Speaking rationally, I should not have done it. Too austere, too hard, unfair on myself. I have never left the house to go to a meeting, to speak at a symposium, to be interviewed without praying that I would find a tangent, an escape from the headlong dive into that reality. But I did it anyway. One can only assume that I could not help myself. Then there were the people. Those at the League, of course. But others too, civil servants, doctors, journalists, who won me over. As soon as you love someone, you are trapped.

Besides, counterbalancing effects appeared from nowhere. I had a telephone call from a press organization and I launched into journalism. There I discovered something my family had not been able to offer me: a feeling of lightness. Everything that I loved under one roof: creation, writing, the department, the team, the company, the research, the fight. And rediscovering the incomparable pleasure of working directly for someone whom I recognized as my boss. I had sailed into the right harbour.

Even so, at the square with the children, I was not like other mothers. Sitting on the bench or on the side of the sand pit, I would watch my Elvire making mud pies and I would let Gauthier suck on his biscuit. If another woman wanted to talk to me, I had only two options: a bright façade which devastated me ('Yes, mine's already

three and a half but she's still frightened of the slide; I
can't believe your little scrap, he's so brave up at the top
of the ladder', etc.) or a truth that was socially
unacceptable ('These are my younger two children. The
elder ones died four years ago.') I would always be out of
place. The working class, immigrants, the self-taught
cranks, the handicapped, the unemployed and grieving
parents are more alike than people think. They have at
least one thing in common: they have to make herculean
efforts to hold a normal, banal, bouncy conversation.
They can think of only one thing: the moment when they
might introduce a sentence about their misfortune.
Thirteen years have passed, and I still cannot last half a
day without evoking my daughters.

I gather that a Mr and Mrs Villemin*, who have read
my testimony taken down by Guillemette de Sairigné†,
would like to meet me: what I talked about was what
they had been through themselves. How I understand
them! And how well I remember certain things they have
said that have appeared here and there. Some that were
stamped with the seal of authenticity, and others that had
obviously been rewritten by coarser pens. We all spot
them, these words. And how I remember my own
longing to meet people . . . Ovid, amongst others! Who
had 'taken down' Niobe's testimony. She was the
daughter of Tantalus and one of the Pleiades. She struts,

---

* Their four year-old son, Grégory, was murdered. Although, there was
no evidence, Mrs Villemin was charged with his murder until the case
was withdrawn. Neither murderer nor a motive were ever found.

† Journalist with *Madame Figaro*

defies the gods with her beautiful hair floating on her shoulders. She has seven daughters and seven sons*.

I am happy, who can deny it?
Who can doubt that my great fortune will continue to
    grow?
It is too great – far, far too great for fate to reverse.

Then a goddess who has only two children decides to pull this madam down a peg or two. She kills her sons one by one.

News of disaster, the sad faces of the people,
Tears of her friends brought home to Niobe
Quick sight of ruin: She stood lost in stupor,
Flushed with dark rage at what had come upon her,
And marvelled at the power of the gods
            . . . she bowed
Over the cooling bodies of her sons.
She kissed them, as if she could give them
A lifetime of kisses in these moments.

But she recovers and boasts again, she is proud and arrogant. She still has seven daughters, and the goddess who wants to quash her has only two children!

---

* These quotes are taken from the story of Niobe from Ovid's *Metamorphoses*, Book IV; translations by Horace Gregory, published by Viking Press in 1958, and by Ted Hughes, published by Faber and Faber in 1997, are quoted here.

Even as she spoke one heard the bowstring's music
Which frightened all except distraught Niobe
Whose very madness cleared her mind of fear.

And the arrows knock down the daughters one by one.
Until only the youngest is left.

                    'O not this smallest,
The youngest one,' she cried. 'Leave her to me
Of all my many, leave this last, this one!'
And as she prayed the one she prayed for died.
. . . Life drained from every part of [Niobe], her tongue
Cleaved to her palate and her pulse-beat stopped:
. . . Yet her eyes still wept, and she was whirled away
In a great wind back to her native country,
Where on a mountain top she weeps and even now
Tears fall in rivulets from a statue's face.

After Mathilde and Elise's death, a Greek friend told
me about this legend. I knew that my father-in-law
would be able to lay his hand on it in an instant in his
library. He immediately gave me his book of Ovid with
this note which has never left its pages since: 'For Vève
(see page 7). It seems such a very small thing to do for
you . . . I would prefer to throw myself into the river
Seine, if it would be of any use.' A few lines on the
headed paper of the Ministry for Foreign Affairs. So,
there we are. Jean-Marie Villemin and my father-in-law
the ambassador, Christine Villemin, Niobe, myself – the
workmen, the bourgeoisie and the demi-gods – we all
have the same story. And we find that it is told better

when it is told by someone else. The more I explain the
less I understand. You yourself felt it when you saw
Elvire playing ping-pong at the stadium 'with a young
girl' – those were your own words – and I told you: 'That
young girl is Aude, the baby who was sleeping in the
Renault 5 with Mathilde and Elise.' You were stupified,
suddenly too close to understand. It is the same for me.
My story is clearer when it is told by Ovid. And the story
of Grégory Villemin seems clearer to his parents when it
is told by me.

Uzès, 11 August 1997

Elvire has received a postcard from a friend
announcing the death of a classmate, the elder sister of a
friend of Gauthier's, in July. I was having a siesta. In my
drowsy state I could hear the voice of my twelve year-old
daughter, talking to her father, respecting her mother's
sleep. 'I'm going to have to tell Gauthier, aren't I?' He
was playing with his cousin. Gauthier does not want to
hear about anything to do with death. So when Elvire
told him he hid his feelings and hardly broke off from his
game, and Elvire was left alone with this news which she
had just learned from one of those holiday cards that
should never give you that sort of news. 'What's going
on?' I asked, pretending to have heard nothing and
feeling sure that Elvire would want to tell me everything
herself.

She joined me on the bed, buried herself against me,
sighed and then cried. She had been telling me about this
friend's illness since the beginning of the school year. I
knew that Laurence came to school sporadically, that she
had changed physically, that her mother, who was always
cheerful, came to pick her up from school with her two
younger children, asking her whether she had forgotten
anything in her locker, as you would to a child who still

has ten or fifteen years of school ahead of them. Then,
that was it. Laurence sank into a coma. Elvire had told
me about that too but now, as she cried, she realized that
she had never imagined that Laurence would actually die.
And this death, this end to everything, this earthly truth
which meant that the child who had been told not to
forget anything in her locker would not begin the next
academic year in three weeks' time, this was so harsh and
so invincible that Elvire had only her tears to link the
two realities: that of a life yesterday, which was complete
even in a state of coma, and death, which was eternal
right from the first moment. Now, even as she struggled
with the sharp pain, she already knew that soon, very
soon, this pain would soften, and despite her sobs, her
shuddering little frame, and her puffy red face, she was
already regretting the purity of this revolt before it had
even begun to fade, and she refused to accept that this
sorrow would become integrated into her life. 'When I
tell my children about this one day, they won't
understand how horrible it was,' she told me. And then:
'Maybe even tomorrow there will already be moments
when I won't think about it.' This idea redoubled her
anger. Far from hoping to suffer less, she never wanted
the freshness of the pain to deaden; this was the only
acceptable response to a disappearance that every part of
her refused to accept. As I listened to her I loved her for
having already understood everything, and I thought of
these letters in which, so many years later, I try to
discover exactly what has become of all those feelings.

12 August 1993

*W*hen a stranger asks me how many children I have
in front of Elvire and Gauthier, I can feel them waiting
for my answer with an almost hostile vigilance. They
know that I am going to lie and answer 'two'. Afterwards
they never fail to ask me why I have once again betrayed
them, betrayed their sisters and betrayed myself. They are
enraged when they see me embroidering the truth like
this. There are four of them. They were born third and
fourth. Only they could say what their sisters mean to
them, if it interested them to try and understand. But
Mathilde and Elise are their sisters, and their elders even
though they have now overtaken them in years on this
earth. And it sickens them to hear me rewriting history
when I fail to admit the most stubborn of realities; I have
four children, three girls and a boy.

At Uzès the other evening Elvire called urgently:
'Come here! Mummy, come here!' I rushed over.
'Mathilde's lampshade is burning,' she told me. Yes, their
bedside light with its music box which plays *A la claire
fontaine* was pressed up against the wall, the shade had
been knocked and it was touching the bulb. I switched
the light off and removed the shade. It had a hole in it, a
gaping hole. This light dated back to one of the older

girls, I would probably have said Elise. The children were
crying. I shrugged my shoulders: 'When the bulb has
cooled down, I'll put the shade back on and turn it round
so that you can't see the hole.' Which I did. And I put
my children to bed. Then, half asleep myself, I tore
myself away from their lovely smell and their sleeping
bodies which were sprawled across mine, to go back to
my own bed. People keep telling me that they are too big
to sleep with me!

Cool sheets, the vast expanse of the double mattress.
Elvire, my Elvire reappeared in my mind as she had been
a few hours previously on the platform at the station in
Avignon, framed in the doorway as she stepped out of
the carriage. She had come back from China, where her
godmother had taken her. On her head she had piled up
the paddy-field hats that she was bringing back for us,
and she smiled at me, giggling, so funny and alive. She
returned from the other side of the world, funny and
alive. 'I love my sister so much,' Gauthier had whispered
as he waited for her. She had been swallowed up among
thousands of millions of Asians for two weeks, and she
had distinguished herself from them to come home. At
home. With her hats. I thought how, thirteen years
earlier, I used to look for my daughters amongst
thousands of millions of strangers. 'If I made all of
humanity, every being one after the other, pass through a
little doorway, I would surely end up seeing Mathilde and
Elise go through . . .' Elvire is here. In the doorway. I fell
asleep. A little girl was running along a road ravaged by
war; she ran naked, crying. I went up to her. 'We've
turned the burnt bit round so that you can't see it,' I told

myself. I come closer. I recognize both my own daughter – but which one? – and the Vietnamese child with the burnt back who fled her burning village during the war.

Elvire told me that at the airport in China her godmother was so afraid of losing her that she had knotted her dress to her god-daughter's T-shirt. An umbilical cord of cotton! How lovely people are!

23 August 1993

I joined my family for one last summer weekend:
Laurent and the children are spending the end of the
month in Uzès. Gauthier showed me the end of his index
finger on his right hand; it was stiff, hot and swollen
because he had been stung by an insect – perhaps a
scorpion, we will never know – when he had poked his
finger into the outside tap. Elvire had made an
arrangement with an elderly man to groom his horse and
feed his chickens morning and evening, in a farmhouse
on the other side of town. The house is full of family,
cousins and dogs. On Saturday we had supper at a
friend's house at the foot of the Pont du Gard. It was a
sparkling and amusing evening, successful authors, film
producers; the stories they told delighted us, we could not
tell the fact from the fiction, at times they got carried
away by their own talent, at others they shared with us
excellent anecdotes which seemed very spicy to people
like us who lead quiet lives. The next day, tennis.
Gauthier was on the other side of the wire fence and he
pressed his cheek up against it so that I could kiss him
when I went to pick up a ball from that side. I kissed
him, I played tennis, and at the same time I thought
about my daughter who would need picking up at

lunchtime from her horses, her donkeys and her chickens, and about what had stayed with me from the previous evening, like the account of Francis Bouygues's* funeral, where the invitations were accompanied by a Bouygues pin badge. Hostesses dressed in black seated you when you arrived at the church. The signs: 'personalities', 'TF1', and the most condemning sign: 'miscellaneous' . . . a funeral cast in concrete. This furious need to be the best at everything. At least so long as you still have control over something! And I was beaten once again! 6/2, 6/1! How long is it now since I won a game of tennis?

Last night Laurent took me to the airport at Nîmes. I love these weekends but it absolutely finishes me when I leave him. When we were still in the car on the road we saw the A320 which was to take me away landing. In the airport there were people waiting for passengers on the incoming flight from Paris. Laurent took my hand-luggage and my ticket so that he could check me in. As I looked round, my eye rested on a very young girl with long blond hair; because of the heat she wore a tiny dress, a veil of fabric over her slender body. She was waiting with a whisper of a smile on her face, Vanessa Paradis but more innocent, Ophelia but more earthly. I told myself she was waiting for the man she loved, and indeed a very young man came towards her; he was tall, long-limbed, slim and dark, and he took her in his arms. They

---

* Francis Bouygues, the director of the massive construction company Bouygues, bought up and managed France's first television channel TF1, which had previously been state owned.

kissed so tenderly, and for so long! Their arms squeezed
round each other's waist, then the neck, then the hips,
then the waist again. I told myself – as I often did – that
there was nothing like the beginnings of a love affair; I
hesitated between my own happy memories and my regret
at knowing what becomes of these delights. I thought of
reunions with Laurent long ago, at Chicago airport. Why
had I gone and weighed my own very young man down
with all these children, and a difficult wife, and
responsibilities, anxieties? And all the time the two
beautiful lovers were still kissing just ten metres away
from me! I also thought that things were not all that
dismal because twenty-three years later I still had a heavy
heart because I was leaving my man for just five days. I
thought back to something I had noticed the previous
evening, during that sparkling dinner: when there are
people gathered together like that, Laurent is never the
one who shows off, tells captivating stories or makes
everyone laugh. But he is always the one who intrigues
them with his vigilant presence, the way he listens kindly,
and leaves the limelight to whoever claims it. All the
same, those lovers were an incredible sight, their hair still
mingling in an endless kiss, apparently unable to leave the
airport. Laurent came back. 'I've taken this out of your
bag, it was too heavy, he wanted to put it in the hold.'
'This' was a steak-pan that I was taking back for my
mother! So there he is, my Laurent, handing me my
luggage and my boarding card, and getting ready to say
goodbye and walk across the hall with this steak pan in
his hand . . . I catch him by his sleeve, tell him we have
time for a cup of coffee, talk to him feverishly, point the

lovers out to him, launch into confused lines of reasoning,
tell him that I hate wives who destroy the men they love,
send them to the supermarket, make them fill the boot of
the car, blackmail them with 'you never do anything with
the children', and there I am leaving him with ours in
Uzès . . . Him: 'I'm sorry, but I'm really worried that
you'll miss your plane. And anyway, I had absolutely no
desire to end up as a cretinous old bachelor.' Me: 'I don't
give a damn about my plane. You could at least have
found yourself a gentle little self-effacing wife who would
have looked after everything while you followed your
destiny.' He gets up and shrugs his shoulders: 'That's the
nineteenth century. It's not what I want at all.' I bundle
the steak pan into my bag. There are limits. We kiss.
Laurent checks that there is nothing that is worrying me.
A last squeeze of the hand and it is over. But at least I
saw him leave with his hands free.

Then on the plane I think about him and the children
and the little path behind the house lined with brambles
where the two of us used to walk at night in the first few
summers, and where, later, with the dog and each of the
four children, I would go to pick blackberries. But when I
got off the plane at Orly, even though no-one knew I
was coming back, I still caught myself sweeping my eye
over the groups of people waiting for passengers.

At home there is no more and no less mess than I left
here on Friday. On the table there are forms to fill in for
the beginning of the school year. Some dates from the
local council to put into my diary. I glanced at the
aquarium and the cage: fish and birds are fine. Gauthier
is going into class CM 2; this will be the last year that I

have a child in primary school. And in five weeks I am
changing jobs. I put the washing-machine on. I only have
a few days left to clean the apartment, fill the fridge and
work through the build-up of paperwork. I go to bed. I
try to remember which nighties and pyjamas Mathilde
and Elise wore right at the very end. In this heat, Elvire
and Gauthier sleep in T-shirts and underpants at Uzès.

When I arrive at the office I am still troubled by this
disjointed life, these separations and contradictions. The
morning ritual of reading the newspapers does nothing to
help. On the shelves there are photographs of my
children. At twelve, nine, seven and four they form a
coherent family. 'Are they your children?' Yes. They are
my children. Except that the younger two are the elder
two, but there is no point in going into details. I now
realize that, since I have been writing to you, I do not
really like talking about my daughters to strangers. I
sometimes try to remember what it was like before I
started writing to you. In my last letter, in which I told
you about Elvire coming home from her trip to the Far
East, it took me a long time to realize that the image of
her in the doorway of the carriage brought back visions of
other homecomings. Ones which will only ever be visions.

I am like Penelope with her tapestry: as long as she
was still working at it, no-one could say that Ulysses
would never come home. With this correspondence, I too
am trying to reunite my family.

Monday, 6 September 1993

A meeting this morning at the Ministry of Transport
in the Grande Arche building. I come out of the *métro*
with a few minutes to spare and wander round the
shopping centre. A record shop: I go over to the section
on Eric Clapton. Just over two years ago I went on a
business trip to the United States with the financial
director of my office. The moment we landed in New
York we saw the newspaper headlines: Eric Clapton's
child, a little two year-old boy, had fallen from a window.
From the twenty-fifth floor, I think. Over the next few
days, in between the seminars, I would go back up to my
hotel room to watch television. To see, to know, to think.
The image of Clapton standing by the grave.

   At the record shop, I look at the dates of the
recordings. I buy a double CD, two hours recorded 'live'
during a recent tour. How do you sing two years
afterwards?

   And in the evening, I listen to it while I do the
ironing. Endless, fastidious guitar solos. Familiar songs
from about twenty years ago. And then 'Tears in
Heaven'. A whispered lullaby accompanied by a crisp
guitar. Bruno, with whom I wrote songs at the beginning
of the year, told me one morning that the previous

evening his sons had asked him to play for them at
bedtime. He had taken his twelve-string guitar and sung
a children's song, 'La Poupée qui fait non'. With the
same intonations that I am listening to now? Singing for
your sons at the foot of their bed. Singing on stage for a
son who fell out of bed.

In his song Clapton asks questions which only a song
would allow him to ask so starkly. 'Would you know my
name if I saw you in heaven? Would you hold my hand?
Would you feel the same? I must be strong 'cause I know
I don't belong here in heaven. I'll find my way through
night and day. Beyond the door there's peace I'm sure.
And I know there'll be no more tears in heaven. I don't
belong here in heaven . . .'

It was the same process as a few years ago when I used
to listen to the *Stabat Mater* written by Dvořák after his
children died, or when I contemplated the *Dead Christ*
painted by Mantegna, who was orphaned by his two sons.
When you have lost a child, all that is left is to try to
understand what you can. Some artists achieve this with
fiction. They are right. In my first novels I showed far
more clearly what I had lost, far more clearly than I am
showing you. Without saying that I had lost it.
Madeleine Chapsal* even reproached me for just that.
But a book is not meant to say everything at once. It is
already an achievement if it says one thing. In his
painting, Mantegna presents Christ from a very unusual
angle, with his feet in the foreground. Probably as he saw

---

* A reviewer and author

his own sons, Federico and Girolamo. And as I did not
see my daughters. And then, at the head of the bed, he
painted himself, stupefied and anguished. He, therefore,
shows what he actually sees, and shows himself as he
imagines himself to be. He shows us the scene and
ponders over his own pain. He is trying to find out who
he is now that his sons are dead.

In 'Tears in Heaven', Clapton tackles the question of
time. He counter-balances the cliché that time heals
everything. 'Time can bring you down, bring you what
you need, Time can break you heart, make you beg and
plead,' he sings. It is true. I knew that straight away. I
lived off my happiness not knowing what I would live off
next.

Bettelheim maintained that the children he saw at the
Orthogenic School, who were so terribly ill, grew up to
be stronger than average because, having overcome the
exhausting struggles against their internal disorders, they
were not going to be intimidated by the everyday
problems in life. Laurent and I both feel like that. One
evening he was alone in the house at Uzès with seven
children. A little girl crushed her finger under a huge
stone in a barn. He told me how he had carried her close
to him, shattered by the sight of this mutilated little hand
but exalted to be taking her to the competent care of
doctors, which he had not had the opportunity to do for
his daughters. Healing, what a comforting activity!

What I am trying to explain to you, therefore, is that
Bettelheim is right but Clapton is too. I come back to the
fall of the empire and the falling of a glove. If you have
withstood the fall of an empire you are invincible. You

know what you can survive. You are strong, you have needed your strength and you are proud of it. The only thing that could drag you under would be a completely different kind of fall. Which plucks you gently. So you fall gently and very far. So gently that you do not make a sound as you touch the bottom. No more sound than you would make if you were to pronounce the word disappearance.

13 September 1993

Upheavals at the office: my friends are packing their cardboard boxes. I have been appointed to another job and I am leaving the development department. My friends are no longer attached to me, they are moving out, setting themselves up in new surroundings. I am taking up my next job in a fortnight. Tomorrow morning Philippe, the artistic director with whom I have worked so closely for four years, will not park his motorbike outside my door. The first question of the day: 'Is Philippe here?' will never be the first question of the day again. I am pleased to be going where I am going. And yet, right up until my friends started packing their boxes, I had not wanted to acknowledge that I would be going without them.

Some pages can be turned quite normally. Without sorrow.

This summer in Uzès, Elvire and Gauthier were looking for a birthday present for their father. What can you find when you are twelve and nine and you only have a few pennies at the bottom of your pocket? Gauthier, who is preoccupied with the idea of identity, and is as passionate about the mystery of people's names as he is about hieroglyphics, chose a key ring which enumerated the characteristics of people called Laurent. Elvire dragged me to the poetry department of a bookshop. 'Lamartine,' she said because she knew that her father had named her after the mistress to whom *Le Lac* is dedicated. But Laurent already had so many different editions! 'Verlaine . . . does he like Verlaine?' Yes. And probably knows his work by heart. She was drawn to a slim anthology: *Wisdom, Love, Happiness.* It was just within her budget. Before wrapping it up she wrote on the first page: 'For my Daddy, who brought me up with wisdom, love and happiness.'

The children once asked me whether my father liked poetry too. Yes, particularly Apollinaire. Thanks to him, for example, he could come closer to natural things, like the heather with which Noirmoutier was carpeted and which reminded him of a poem which he used to recite

to Christine and myself when we were little. I recited it
to them:

I have picked this sprig of heather
The autumn is dead, remember
We will not meet again on this earth
The smell of the weather, the sprig of heather
*And I wait for you, remember**

They made no comment. What adieux did it evoke for
them? I was quiet too, thinking that, by reciting those
verses to us, my father might already have been preparing
to say goodbye to us. How lucky to be able to prepare
oneself.

We were given the opportunity to go for a holiday
together this autumn. We chose Canada to marvel at the
golden maples. And from there we could go down to
Chicago to show the children our very first student
apartment in the Italian and Yugoslav quarter near the
campus where Laurent had been a student. I would take
the opportunity to see Bettelheim's school.

And so it was that, travelling along the great lakes,
across the forests, by car and then by train, we slowly
retraced our steps twenty-one years later. In the lecture
theatre Laurent walked between the desks of the students
who had come after him. The children looked at the
architectural models. Their father explained to them the
love of architecture which had sustained him, the work of

* 'L'Adieu' by Guillaume Apollinaire

Mies van der Rohe, glass, metal, sobriety, external
structures that liberate the internal space, the philosophy
of 'less is more'.

And our little flight of steps behind the White Sox
stadium.

When we arrived at the Orthogenic School, I did not
feel well; I looked at the yellow door to which, as a
young therapist, I had held the key for nearly two years.
The lantern, the window of Bettelheim's office on the
right. Behind the curtain of the left-hand window the
doll's house had not moved. But I ran away, I did not
want to be photographed there. I had been expecting
Mathilde last time I had crossed that door. At the time
we took life on so willingly.

We went to have lunch in an Italian restaurant. I was
haunted by a tune, a song from that era, Joan Baez or
Bob Dylan. Not that I ever much liked either of those
two, mind you. Why was it going round in my head? I
could not get rid of it. And then the words came back to
me: 'Where have you been, my blue-eyed son, oh where
have you been, my darling young one . . .'

I thought of my correspondent, of Paris, of all those
letters written to discover where my 'darling young ones'
had gone. The question was still virgin territory. Nothing
had been said. The four of us were in Chicago – Laurent,
Elvire, Gauthier and myself. The six of us would never be
there together. I would have to start all over again, write
a thousand more letters. But I bought a simple postcard
to tell our friend that we were having a lovely holiday and
sent him lots of love.